D/2024/45/270 – ISBN 978 94 014 2941 2 – NUR 800

Design illustration cover: Mieke Geenen
Design cover: Peer Demaeyer
Design interior: Keppie & Keppie

LannooCampus Publishers is a subsidiary of Lannoo Publishers,
the book and multimedia division of Lannoo Publishers nv.

LannooCampus Publishers
Vaartkom 41 box 01.02
3000 Leuven
Belgium

P.O. Box 23202
1100 DS Amsterdam
The Netherlands

www.lannoocampus.com

PROVO TYPING

STEFAAN VANDIST

DEVELOP
AND REALISE
SUSTAINABLE
FUTURE VISIONS

Lannoo
Campus

For Juliette, Casper,
everyone and everything that lives,
the approximately 7.8 million species
on earth, today,
and the many generations that follow.

CONTENTS

Provotyping

*Developing and realising sustainable
visions of the future*

Bet: Provocative prototyping

provotipə]
/ˈprəʊtətaɪp/
Pro-vo-type

'Whatever you can do,
or dream you can, begin with it.
Boldness has genius,
power and magic in it.'

———

JOHANN WOLFGANG GOETHE

THE BIG DATA TRILOGY: EXPERIENCE, ENGAGEMENT AND ENCHANTMENT

It's September 2020, and when you enter the theatre in cultural centre *C-Mine* in Genk, you immediately feel that *BIAS* is not going to be your average theatre performance. A queue of actors with laptops and question-naires at the ready serves the audience with labels, just as algorithms do with people on a daily basis on the internet. Once inside, you will be confronted with a large chalkboard with names of participants and traits such as *Friend-ly, Hairy, Open-minded, Arrogant, Old, Fat, Dark, Pretty, Young,* ... are connected in a complex interplay of lines. There is also a large disc-shaped figure drawn that is reminiscent of the game show *Wheel Of Fortune*.

Indeed, the performance begins with the jolly atmosphere of a game show from the nineties. You have to be careful, because you will receive sharp instructions on how to engage in interviews with other participants and how to share them with the actors, who record everything accurately. The conver-sations have something of *speed dating*, and that often leads to laughter in the room. An old lady, a young skater... The crazier the match with another participant who sits in front of me, the more fun. But am I doing this right? Is it for points? The presenter reveals that the ultimate society is being cre-ated here. Based on Big Data and Artificial Intelligence, this should create a perfectly matching group of people.

A few times the game is stopped and A.I. indicates which people have to leave. We end up with a handful of people. The final outcome is supposed to be perfect. We have all worked towards it, and all feel slightly enchanted by that invisible finger that has determined our route. But at the same time, we feel gloomy and empty: The crazy guys who had to leave were the ones who gave colour to the evening.

BIAS was the second performance in the *Big Data Trilogy* by the Playfield theatre company. It made people feel deep down what we all know by now: artificial intelligence parrots our prejudices in a digital echo chamber, and that requires caution if we hope to use it to build important social structures. You can write test pieces or opinion pieces about it, but it only really sinks in when you experience it *firsthand*.

In this book I take you on a pilgrimage in search of experiences that broaden your view and ways you can create them yourself and use them strategically to shape your future. Provotyping is both a methodology and a call to appeal to our imagination, to develop a vision, to bring together a vanguard of organisations around us and to provoke engagement by translating that vision into an experience that will resonate for a long time to come. This is the only way we can take control of our own story about the future.

From the old normal
to the new sublime.

'Tell me, and I'll forget.
Show me and maybe I'll remember,
but involve me and I'll learn.'

———

BENJAMIN FRANKLIN

WHAT IF?

COALITION
OF THE WILLING

PROVOTYPING

CELEBRATION

THIS BOOK IN SHORT

FROM THE OLD NORMAL TO THE NEW SUBLIME

In these turbulent times in which the restoration of our broken connection with nature, society and ourselves is central, there is a poignant lack of imagination. We experience that the current story is no longer sufficient to bring about a hopeful (let alone exciting) future. The world is crying out for a new, grand story to believe in. Fortunately, the script for this story can come from the bundling of numerous large and small initiatives. Provotyping is both a call and a methodology not to settle for a supporting role, but to claim the leading role in a future-inspired narrative that we make tangible and visible in four steps.

 ## WHAT IF?

The seed of everything lies in the unfolding of an attractive and connecting vision of the future. A stimulating look at the future is more powerful than numbers and statistics. It puts our motives under the right tension and offers a dot on the horizon. With a guiding vision of the future, the narrative of your organisation or initiative can take shape step by step.

 ## COALITION OF THE WILLING

You will soon need that vision of the future in order to cultivate an 'alliance of the willing' around it. Work together with people and organisations within and outside your sector who have an interest in achieving that same vision of the future. No matter the size of your organisation, you can't change the world on your own. With a 'coalition of the willing' you create your own power of change to rewrite the rules of the game.

#3 PROVOTYPING

Free that beautiful vision of the future from the meeting room as soon as possible. So that people can really experience it, we translate it into a visible and tangible 'provocative prototype': We gently do violence to the existing, and hold up the mirror to something new. Add some wonder to the experience and magic happens: you open minds to renewal and turn on the creative light.

People are going to get it as soon as they see it.

#4 CELEBRATION

In a communication universe where the future is often trapped in doomsday scenarios, dry reports and technical terms, I want to argue for a radically different approach: celebrating. Celebrating new insights and breakthroughs thanks to Provotyping throws a shining light on the way forward. As soon as there is something to celebrate, everyone likes to come and be under the spotlight. Celebration resonates deep in our hearts, so make sure to applaud everyone.

With this book I address the fast-growing group of *impact professionals*. People for whom work, innovation, education, technology, science and entrepreneurship not only lead to profit, but also to the growth of social, environmental and cultural capital.

In a process of Provotyping, I want to pave the way with them. A path from the old normal to the new sublime.

QR code to digital
Provotyping Canvas

'You are what you do,
not what you say you do.'

———

CARL JUNG

7 REASONS WHY SUSTAINABILITY DOESN'T WORK

No sane person can object to an ecological and social future. Never has there been so much international connection and engagement around climate goals. So why does it seem so difficult to turn the tide? Here are seven obstacles that I often see organisations, teams and managers encounter. Each time with the beginning of a solution.

THE WORD 'SUSTAINABILITY' ITSELF

When it comes to sustainability, the word 'expensive' doesn't just stand out in the supermarket. Also from a social point of view, it is the absolute elephant in the room. Sustainability policy is skewed at the upper middle class and is too often limited to subsidies for electric cars and solar panels.

Public transport, draughty and poorly insulated social housing receive far too little attention. Sociologist and poverty expert Wim Van Lancker (KU Leuven) strongly emphasises that the poorest bear the least responsibility, but are hit the hardest. A positive turnaround would be that revenues from CO_2 taxes, often collected at the top of the social ladder, would be collectively invested at the bottom with scalable solutions. The most vulnerable people in society should be the first to experience the benefits. That's the only way we're going to get everyone on board.

Today, the rigid and over-used concept of 'sustainability' is accelerating to the much more dynamic term 'regenerative', and that is a necessary reset in our systems thinking. Sustainability is essentially about efforts to make what is there last longer. Regenerative design is about creating conditions in which every activity always contributes to restoration, renewal, enrichment and balance of ecological systems and social structures.

THE IDEOLOGICAL ARM WRESTLE

Since its inception in the US in the late 1960s, the environmental movement has been divided into two camps: those who believe that we need to return to a harmonious balance with nature, and those who are convinced that science and technology will always help us avoid disaster. More than fifty years later, our future is still held hostage by an arm-wrestle for some great ideological right. One sows fear that a low-carbon society will cost too much, while the other points to the backlog and missed opportunities if it is not invested in more quickly. Green growth, regrowth, degrowth… In this book, it will often become clear that striving to be right is of little value.

What counts today is moving forward together. A good medicine against the inhibiting effect of ideological contradictions is creativity. With creativity, you can show solutions where traditional opposites are absorbed by the magical appeal of something new that doesn't fit into a plus or minus box.

WE ARE F.U.C.D.

Perhaps sustainability, especially in the climate aspect, deserves the prize for the most depressing story ever: A disaster of unprecedented scale, too complex to understand, in which hardly anyone seems to be able to make a difference, yet everyone – including you – is guilty. This leads to total FUCD, or feelings of fear, uncertainty, cynicism and doubt, and that's a shame, because it's the ideal recipe for making us completely switch off mentally. Shauna Moran, trend researcher at the international market research agency GWI, talks about apocalypse fatigue: the effect of constant 'final warnings' and the persistent moral appeal to make choices where the result is barely visible or tangible. Of course, the task is of enormous scale. Our annual global CO_2 emissions of 38 gigatonnes per year alone are the equivalent of a lump of coal the size of a football stadium going up in the air every second. Moreover, all global challenges such as climate, biodiversity, food security, inequality, democracy and geopolitical stability are increasingly intertwined like a cluster f*ck. With a polite word, it is sometimes called the *polycrisis* and that weighs on our mental health.

Replace the vague climate frame with a framework with exciting, achievable and feasible perspectives. Regenerative agriculture, shared transport, a circular construction sector, bio-based materials... Each and every one of them is a challenging assignment in which the unique assets of a region can be exploited and in which entrepreneurs, active citizens or professionals can join with the best of themselves.

A CRISIS OF IMAGINATION

'If progress has no story, the past tells where we are going', was the title of the column by Rob Wijnberg, founder of *De Correspondent* the morning after Geert Wilders' victory (Dutch parliamentary elections, 2023). I myself also occasionally make myself unpopular in progressive circles by arguing that the progress of the populist right has not only to do with the resonance of their *nostalgic nationalism* (progress is something that takes you back to supposedly better times), but also because of the chronic failure of the progressive wing to promote a convincing prospect of how the world can be fundamentally better. The dominant socio-ecological narrative is about less-less-less: consume less, travel less, less space, etc. But progress requires an exciting story of abundant possibilities: greater quality of life, better health and more opportunities to make your dreams come true.

NON-COMMITTAL BLUFFING CRIES

The concept of purpose has occupied a prominent place in the canon of management buzzwords over the past decade. Brands quantify their return-on-purpose after throwing big ideals into the marketing mix. The impact of the higher-purpose economy is proving to be very lucrative, as Deloitte demonstrated once again in 2023: meaning-driven brands capture a larger market share, typically grow three times faster, show 30% better innovation performance, and retain their talent better. The desire for meaning is a need to be marketed.

Despite all the good, there is one point of attention that we should not ignore. Organisations can choose that Greater Ideal strategically, comfortably and according to their own interests. And most of the time, they ignore the real structural pain points that a sector should be facing.

A major bank can sponsor the nation's largest charity show and shine with its support for disadvantaged groups, so as not to have to talk about systemic failures that perpetuate financial inequality. Fashion giants can refresh their image with colourful stories that embrace the LGBTIQA+ movement, diverting attention from distressing working conditions and ecocide in fragile ecosystems.

In the coming years, we are facing a tsunami of new regulations that should provide society with a more ecological, social and future-proof model. Greenwashing and other forms of superficial purpose marketing will decrease in effectiveness and even be legally restricted. Armies of consultants are being groomed to guide companies through these new legislative frameworks, particularly around ESG (Environmental, Social and Governance) and the CSRD (Corporate Sustainability Reporting Directive).

CHECKLIST SUSTAINABILITY

It is a big leap forward to set up systems to assess what matters and for organisations to use the same metrics and scoreboards for this. But it is crucial not to fall into a reissue of *'checklist sustainability'* where sustainability is reduced to norms, figures and statistics. We need to avoid getting bogged down in sustainability incrementalism (mistaking small, quantifiable improvements in the margins, thus denying us the space for real, transformative changes). The future must not only be the work of a new professional group that will populate a recently inaugurated accounting department for sustainability. It should be a cultural challenge and innovation task that is at the top of everyone's curriculum.

A BROKEN FUTURE NARRATIVE

Every good story contains suspense, a relatable hero, captivating obstacles, and a goal to strive for. People all over the world love stories. We are all the product of the stories we are part of and that we talk ourselves into. A major reason why our current narrative falls short is because we have less and less faith that it will bring us an exciting future. We increasingly feel reduced to consumers and 'human resources' that benefit a small elite and saddle society with rising costs, and an imminent climate catastrophe.

If we don't change that script, we'll end up as bored and annoyed actors in a sad storyline. A boring story of success and social status, according to behavioural psychologist Tom De Bruyne. There are many epic adventures waiting for us, but we are mainly urged to sort waste, consume less and spend money on an electric car.

According to research by
the Stockholm Resilience Centre (2024),
83% of citizens in G20 countries want to make efforts
to become better guardians of the planet.

As the world slowly turns into Instagram, we should experience it more like Minecraft, a game where people are encouraged to work together to create beautiful new worlds.

The good thing is that the new story that people are longing for consists of the sum and connection of many large and small stories, and more and more organisations are composing a new story in which citizens and consumers are reserved a first-class place to play a nice role in.

'If we want to cool the planet,
we will first have to warm people's hearts.'

1

7 + 1 SUPER-POWERS

In the messy and sloshing dynamics of change, forces are manifesting themselves that are irreversibly transforming the world: climate change, geopolitical changes, ageing populations, the rise of exponential technology, ... They are all autonomous developments that permeate and shape the fabric of our society. As an individual, it sometimes seems an impregnable task to comprehend, let alone direct, these cosmic flows.

Still, in this part, we explore seven superpowers that are within reach of everyone, ready to be deployed by impact professionals. Each and every one of them are the essential practical tools in the toolbox of those who do not want to passively ride the waves of our time, but who want to actively navigate and shape.

7 + 1 INSTRUMENTS

1 **Storytelling:** With the power of story, you help understand and change the world. Stories connect facts and emotions and are the key to understanding and engagement.

2 **Wonder:** Opens the gates to new perspectives and creative possibilities, a breeding ground for innovation and renewal.

3 **Inspiration from nature:** There are timeless lessons in the rich palette of flora and fauna. Nature is an inexhaustible source of inspiration for sustainable change.

4 **New technology:** Technology has always been a kind of self-portrait of civilisation and the catalyst for progress. Never before has technology been at the fingertips of so many people. You'll find the tools to transform the world.

5 **Knowledge of new legislation:** Acts as a map and compass in the complex landscape of regulations, allowing it to operate within its borders with room for positive impact.

6 **Creative collaboration:** Recognising that the sum of diverse talents and perspectives is greater than the individual parts is a driving force for collective innovation.

7 **Well-being in the workplace:** Nothing is as strong as a good team of people who feel good about themselves and together create a creative and constructive organisational culture.

8 **Impact investment:** Conscious investments and new ownership structures are levers for social change where you can give more space to social inclusion and ecological balance.

'Sustainability is forever migrating
from "the land of promise"
to "the land of proof".'

How do we serve the future with a new story that is attractive and connecting, and to which people can contribute with the best of themselves?

HOMO NARRANS

Put a human with a chimpanzee, gorilla or baboon in a boxing ring, and the human will be on the ropes in no time. Yet it is homo sapiens who, in the blink of an eye, has taken control of our planet as an upright walking primate. Not because we can run faster, nor because of our muscle strength, but because of our ability to tell stories and work together. No one explains better than Yuval Noah Harari (Sapiens, 2011) how the foundations of civilisation arose from our ability to believe in grand narratives. We produce knowledge, create abstract ideas and stories, prod ourselves and each other to believe in them, and regularly succeed in making them real. You can use it to found world religions, build cities and settle wars. Over the past 2,000 years, stories have often paid homage to god, money, or nation-states.

Stories are the mental post-it notes that allow you to stick ideas and beliefs into people's heads. Because our brain uses a lot of energy, it quickly goes into hibernation mode when you feed it with all too predictable things. Our brain is allergic to boredom and therefore likes to be entertained. As a storyteller, the amygdala, not much bigger than an almond nut – is your best friend. The amygdala is part of your limbic system and is involved in emotions, motivation, learning, and memory storage. A storyteller sits at a button table like a kind of DJ and gets the happiness hormones dancing. You serve your audience with Dopamine, Oxytocin, Serotonin and Endorphins (D.O.S.E. for short), four neurotransmitters that largely determine how we feel.

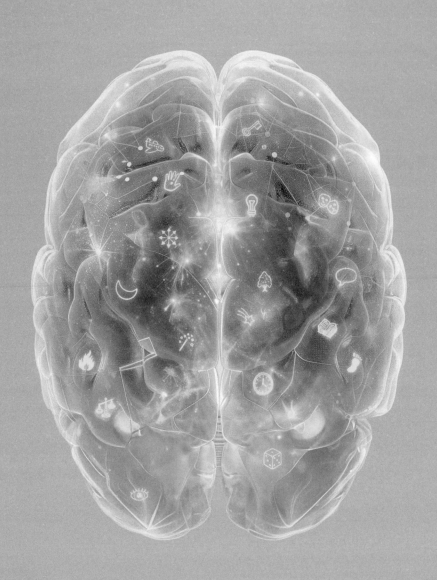

With stories, you can:

1 spark people's imaginations;
2 make the most unthinkable tangible;
3 make complexity manageable;
4 stimulate people with what is desirable and possible;
5 ignite the inner fire;
6 unite and engage people around new ideas;
7 start a movement;
8 and motivate people to keep going.

The list above suggests that storytelling offers the ultimate *playbook* to connect people in, say, the fight against climate change. But when it comes to our future – at the breakfast table, at the coffee machine in the office, or on a TV talk show – it often seems as if we are completely *FUCD* (Fearful, Uncertain, Cynical and Doubtful). More than ever, the future is filled with feelings of fear, uncertainty, cynicism and doubt when it should be a story of hope, possibilities and opportunity. For 23 years in a row, the annual Edelman Trust Barometer – an international survey of trust in society – has shown that trust in political institutions, companies and the media to manage our future is becoming increasingly fragile.

TECHNICALITIES UNDER THE HOOD

If there's one thing we need to rewrite, it's our story about the future, and about sustainability in particular. During lectures, I often do a thought experiment with the audience to demonstrate this. I ask them to put themselves in the shoes of a car salesman in a showroom. Completely in the spirit of Jordan Belfort's (better known as *The Wolf of Wall Street*) sales training, I ask 'sell this car'. I give two options:

1 You try to impress your customer with all the special features of this car and the superior technicalities under the hood.
2 You try to find out your customer's dreams for the future with empathy, and let that car play a very important role in that.

Whatever the composition of the audience, almost all hands invariably go up in the air for the second strategy. You have to make sure that the customer likes to see themselves in that car. Then he will automatically come up with the rational arguments to justify that purchase. So apparently we know very well how behavioural control works (in this case: coughing up a large amount of money for a new car). And so we know that this process is not based purely on rational arguments. But as soon as we want to sell more care for climate or biodiversity, we invariably dig up figures, statistics and rational arguments. Few organisations succeed in packaging their sustainability story into an attractive vision of the future in which their products, services or customers and their new behavioural habits play a very decisive role. And that is exactly what we have to do. One scale level higher, a new kind of overarching story is needed that consists of the connection and sum of many large and small stories. This is the only way we can inspire every person or organisation to contribute to the greatest adventure of our time: the transition to a socially inclusive and ecological society. Because the stories we tell each other and ourselves shape our reality. Historian Philipp Blom cheerfully turns this insight on its head without losing its power: stories hold society together as a binding agent, until people have experiences that contradict what they think they know. Then the story starts to waver and it's time for something new.

POST-PURPOSE COMMUNICATION

More and more companies consider positive impact at least as important as financial return and are starting to do very daring things in the process. Some companies give nature and minority groups a formal voice in the boardroom. Beauty company Faith in Nature did this by hiring a director who represents nature on its board of directors. Others are going to entrust their intellectual property to a foundation and embrace new forms of ownership such as *steward ownership*. Yvon Chouinard, founder of clothing brand Patagonia, donated his entire company to a foundation to ensure that every dollar not invested in Patagonia would be paid out as a dividend for nature. In creative incubators for start-ups, marketing and innovation departments, more and more 'post-purpose' thinking is being done. Instead of shining the light on their own greater ideal, which has become an advertising concept, they are going to come up with solutions that citizens and consumers can use to create a better world themselves. The major challengers in the energy sector are therefore no longer talking about their purpose 'climate neutral' or '*the energy system of the future*', because then we are talking about a solution that we can wait another 25 years for. They talk about an *'energy system for the future'*, and started working on it yesterday.

Their marketing consists of the very first step that you, as a citizen consumer, can already subscribe to. *Bolt Energie* is a great Belgian platform that connects energy consumers with local producers of renewable energy without an intermediary. The German company Sonnen has the ambition to become the largest virtual power plant in Europe by connecting 100,000 home batteries to an intelligent network thus remotely absorbing peaks in energy demand. Users share in the profits.

During that trip, citizens, consumers and employees will receive a full seat in first class. Communication about future-proofing is – finally – becoming less formal and decent. In the fight against sustainability fatigue, storytelling goes beyond good goal marketing or far off vague goal formulation. There is a lot of creative experimentation with merciless honesty, humour and the ironic exposé of traditional, outdated practices. The marketing team of the plant-based milk company Oatly seems to have thrown out all the marketing books and always stands out with 'brutally honest campaigns'. From 'It's like milk, but for people' to empty advertising space that is donated to traditional dairy companies so that they too can display their ecological footprint. On their website FckOatly, they expertly put all their historical blunders and missteps on a timeline to make it as easy as possible for their opponents.

Not only the challengers to the status quo, but also established companies are increasingly turning to spicy storytelling to mark their transformation. For example, the Swedish energy company Vattenfall made a parody of cinematographic perfume advertising entitled *Industrial Emissions Face Mist*. With top model Cara Delevingne and a perfume based on their emissions that consist only of water, it managed to promote the hydrogen economy in a comical way.

We invent new stories, and then the stories shape us. How can we create a story that gives people space to find their own roles?

Whether you're developing your story for a TED talk, sculpting a story to
convince investors or as a binding agent for your sustainability report:
you develop a story like a chef coming up with a new recipe with special
ingredients.

As for the ingredients, you go in search of a setting, a hero (you, your product or your customer?) a greater ideal (or existential pain), ... You need an
antagonist (a villain, a challenge, or something that upsets balance, ...) You
make style choices, you build structure, you provide surprising elements, you
use strong metaphors, ... But at the base, you need a strong core strategic idea
for your story. *Ratatouille* (Pixar Animation Studio, 2007) wouldn't have been
an interesting film if it was about a rat that likes to cook for the other rats in
the sewer. That wouldn't have been a strong core idea. *Ratatouille* is about the
pain you feel when your dreams are very big (becoming a top chef in a Paris-
ian restaurant) and the effort it takes to break free from your environment (a
colony of garbage and fast food eating rats). It's about a transformation. *Finding Nemo* (Pixar Animation Studio, 2003) could have been a boring film about
fish trying to escape from sharks. But the film is once again about something
much more universal. It's about growing up and breaking free from overpro-
tective parents. Once again, a transformation is at the root of the process.

When I support people in developing their story, I almost always see that
they go berserk in scraping together as much figures, jargon and schematic
representations as possible to substantiate their expertise. I always challenge
them to first determine the absolute core idea of their story. When it comes to
a story about impact, it's good if your core idea contributes to a large, desirable transformation in a smart way. Just think of energy transition, social
inclusion, regenerative food production, the modal shift in mobility from car
traffic to alternatives, and so on... When your solution contributes to this and
runs in the gearbox of the economy with a revenue model, you are automatically relevant. Everything you say, every action, every piece of information
should be a narrative building block that reinforces your core idea.

BioOrg, a biotech start-up in Niel, Antwerp, is developing bacteria that can improve the air quality in buildings. There is the story about the science and technology behind spreading the right microorganisms in buildings, how these creatures neutralise allergens, fine dust and odours as a kind of microbial cleaning team, why that has a beneficial effect on labour productivity, why it is better than cleaning with toxic chemicals, why you waste less water, reduce maintenance costs, which organisations already rely on BioOrg's solutions and so on... All valuable material and all demonstrable with figures, statistics and schemes.

What BioOrg needed was an overarching core idea that was compelling to tell and simple to understand. After a workshop on the recipes and ingredients of storytelling, BioOrg came to the conclusion that it provides buildings with an immune system. The immune system became the core idea. Not only did this seem like a correct, central metaphor for the products, it also resulted in an attractive visual language, and a sustainability story that resonates well in a zeitgeist of green buildings and an increased focus on well-being and health at work.

Sooner or later, everything is a story. Your career, your relationship, the company you founded, what exactly inspired you... One of the best questions you can ask is: how are my people and customers going to tell my story to others? And how are my children and grandchildren going to do that? What transformation have I contributed to? And what was the core idea?

HOW CAN WE ...

- How can we respond to citizens' concerns in our consumer products and services?
- How do our activities contribute to an attractive and connecting story of the future that many people long for?
- How can we transcend numbers and statistics and create a story in which the audience can find its own role?
- How can we put an important societal transformation at the heart of our story? What is our core idea?

Instead of fear, uncertainty and doubt, how can we handle the emotional palette of wonder and enchantment? And why do we need to involve more artists and creatives?

HARVESTING WATER FROM HOT AIR

Imagine an ice-cold can of beer or soda sitting outside on a hot day. Physics treats you to a powerful image that has been used in commercials for decades: the can starts to sweat. In thirsty weather, the cold can will attract humidity and droplets of condensation will bead over the can. Can you build water-producing glaciers in the desert in this way and thus improve the living conditions for millions of people in the world? Can we make food production possible where it is unthinkable today? That's what the Limburg artist Ap Verheggen must have wondered. The phenomenon inspired him to design his *SunGlacier*. Thanks to solar panels and ice packs that work together to attract water molecules from the air, his solar glacier can harvest buckets of fresh drinking water from bone-dry desert air. Verheggen's work aims to encourage people to make the unthinkable tangible in our fight against the effects of climate change.

"There are still so many opportunities in the intersection of art and technology, and people only believe it when they see it. That's why I think Art should give you a kick," says Ap Verheggen.

On November 3, 2021, during the opening of the Dutch pavilion at the World Expo in Dubai, the SunGlacier was a top attraction. The sky was steel blue and shortly after sunrise it was already 33°C warm. A group of dignitaries, including the Dutch royal couple, made their appearance and were given an umbrella in their hands. They were ushered into a domed chapel where ice-cold jets of water rained down from the roof. Amazement all around. Forming a circle around a fresh rainstorm in a space that feels like the Roman Pantheon must have been an almost-religious experience for many. Verheggen shared this enchanting experience with some 950,000 people in the weeks that followed. Behind the scenes, the solar glacier was running at full speed in a six-metre-long shipping container and produced about 1,200 litres of drinking water per day.

THE EIGHT WONDERS OF LIFE

Wonder is a powerful emotion, but it's hard to fathom. Butterflies in your stomach are almost impossible to measure. In their book *Awe, The New Science of Everyday Wonder and How It Can Transform Your Life* (2013), Dr Dacher Keltner and Professor Yang Bai explore where the sensation of wonder comes from and how to get started with it. Putting people in a state of wonder has a number of particularly interesting effects:

EFFECTS OF WONDER

- When we are in wonder, we embrace the unknown and are much more open to new ideas.
- Wonder creates more connection with the outside world and empathy with the people and the world around us. Our *circle of care* is expanding.
- In a state of wonder, you are much less likely to take yourself as a starting point. Your 'ego' and your internal critic are silenced. You are entering an *'ocean of we'*.
- Wonder is good for your emotional flexibility, resilience, and therefore mental health.

75% of us need more moments of wonder.

75% of people report a need for more moments of wonder and awe, and report longing for joy, fun, a touch of mystery, and the virtue of goosebump moments. In uncertain times, the desire for sensations in which we feel intensely alive turns out to be great. Despite the fact that marketing symposia have been talking about 'customer experience' for more than twenty years, 70% of people say they can't remember any exciting initiatives from companies or brands.

'Wonder is the sensation you feel
in the presence of something big
that transforms your understanding
of the world around you.'

———

DR DACHER KELTNER

But what exactly is wonder? Dr Dacher Keltner defines wonder as follows:
Wonder is the sensation you feel in the presence of something great that
transforms your understanding of the world around you.

To better understand what exactly baffles you, Dr Dacher Keltner and Professor Yang asked 2,800 people around the world to write down an experience
full of wonder. People from different generations, from different demograph-
ic, religious, and cultural backgrounds shared their personal testimonies.
The processing of these many stories led to the book *a taxonomy of experiences*
they have called the 'Eight Wonders of Life'.

1 **Moral Beauty**
   Good news for any impact professional: Around the world, stories that
   testify to moral beauty resonate the most. Stories of courage, charity,
   self-sacrifice, perseverance, and leadership that move and inspire us
   to be better people move everyone.

2 **Collective Ecstasy**
   A *Mexican wave* in a football stadium, a well-timed drop during
   a DJ set, or holding a minute's silence in a packed conference room
   to say goodbye to fossil fuels... Collective ecstasy is often hailed
   as the emotional core of religious experiences. Since time immemorial, collective euphoria has provided an uplifting sense of unity
   and connection.

3 **Majestic Nature**
   Nature can both frighten and delight us. In either case, we can be
   overcome by a deep sense of awe and respect. All over the world,
   people recognise that contact with nature can lead to a deep experience of wonder.

4 **The Harmony of Music**
   From didgeridoo to Rachmaninoff ... Music has the magical ability to
   transport us to new dimensions of symbolism and meaning.

5 **Visual Enchantment**
   From painting to architecture... Plastic arts can have an effect of awe
   and bewilderment on people.

6 **Mystical**
People all over the world testify to feelings of wonder and transcend-ence in religious experiences, meditation, prayer and spiritual rituals.

7 **Embracing Life and Death**
In addition to sadness or joy, many people testify to a transcendent experience when they witness a birth, or when they say goodbye to people.

8 **The Satori moment**
Epiphany in English, or the 'snap sensation'. Even if you don't like math, there is that moment when you suddenly understand that equation and you have a euphoric experience of how the puzzle suddenly comes together. Experiencing the coherence of things also leads to sensations of wonder in science.

*'Expectation narrows your view
to what you know, desire, and leads to satisfaction,
disappointment, embrace or rejection...
Wonder opens your gaze curiously to what is there,
leads to seeing, being seen and discoveries.'*

———

BINU SINGH, CHILD PSYCHIATRIST, UZ LEUVEN

ARTISTS IN YOUR STRATEGIC TEAM

In *The Climate Book* (2022) by Greta Thunberg and 200 scientists, global warming sends shivers down your spine, but with all due respect to her com-mitment: I don't believe in the lukewarm recipe of even more information and dialogue to encourage citizens to change their behaviour. By treating them to an authentic experience that moves, they start to feel a much deeper emotional connection to a place, a theme, a challenge or a new idea. This creates resonance. Wonder is an important emotion to activate. Wonder is the field of work of people with a creative brain. That's why it's good to involve creatives, designers and artists in your strategic challenges. Artists have the special characteristic that they often function well in chaos and scarcity. Moreover, they are not easily hindered by rigid structures such as economic business models and scientific conventions, according to jazz guitarist, tech entrepreneur and good friend Arash Aazami.

Artist Ap Verheggen's rain machine didn't happen overnight. Eighty test setups have been completed. The machine travelled with the Dutch armed forces to Mali to determine that things had to be completely different. But today, greenhouse builders want to get started with it and refrigeration companies are building climate labs to experiment with it. The machine was patented, and today SunGlacier is a company that was born out of conviction and wonder: "Everywhere in the world there is light, air and gravity. So you should be able to make water wherever it is needed," says Ap Verheggen.

HOW CAN WE ...

- Which glasses are you wearing? The one of expectation? Or that of wonder?
- And how can we, as entrepreneurs and as a team, further break free from our expectations and embrace many more feelings of wonder?
- Inspired by the Eight Wonders of Life, can you also nurture the interaction with your audience? How are you able to create authentic experiences that move with your vision and offering?
- And do you dare to involve designers and artists to broaden your view of the world?

Nature is a laboratory where 3.8 billion years of evolution have already provided many solutions to today's challenges. How can we get started with the inspiration, the building blocks and the system models that nature generously reveals?

EARTHRISE

William Anders, the youngest of the three-person astronaut trio Frank, Jim and William, secretly smuggled his camera aboard the Saturn V rocket at the launch of NASA's Apollo 8 mission. On Christmas Eve 1968, during the six-day orbit around the moon, Bill, as he was called by friends, took the very first snapshot of Earth: Earthrise. An iconic image of an 'earth rise' that changed our collective self-image forever and confronted us with the limits of our home planet.

The face of our planet – referred to by psychologist Frank White as 'the overview effect' – is a *'cognitive shift'* that affects almost everyone who observes our planet from a lonely distance. The overview effect brings with it an overwhelming sense of enchantment, love, awe, and connection. This explains why a life as an astronaut is often followed by a second career as a climate ambassador or godparent of a nature society.

A PERSONAL OVERVIEW EFFECT

The overview effect has inspired the multi-award-winning organisation Spacebuzz to assemble its own Apollo 8 rockets and hoist them onto trucks. With a simulated space journey in 4D, Virtual Reality glasses and educational packages as luggage, they drive into schoolyards all over the world with the mission: to treat 100 million children to that overview experience.

For a transcendental experience imbued with wonder for the earth can cause a real, lasting *'spirit quake'*. Many entrepreneurs who make revolutionary changes in their organisations out of concern for the future testify that breathtaking experiences of nature, poignant confrontations with the fragility of life, or other miracles of life have played a role in this.

*How can we serve people
with such a satori moment that changes
their perspective on life forever?*

For me, the love for nature arose in my early childhood during sweltering summers in frog pools or balancing on breakwaters at low tide. The water surface in a rock pool acted as a kind of gateway to another world, and staring at everything that moved, I merged with my surroundings, lost all sense of time and space, and experienced my own 'overview effect' on a small scale. This early moment was the seed for what later became my life's mission: to inspire and involve as many people as possible in the greatest adventure of our time: the transition to an inclusive and ecological society.

Every now and then I feel that deep resonance with nature again. When I'm strolling through a dune landscape, working in my garden, pruning plants in my aquariums, or the one time a year when I travel – alone or in a group – to an exotic island to do coral *gardening*.

Coral gardening is the protection, restoration or recreation of endangered coral reefs by means of various techniques, so that this special ecosystem continues to exist for generations to come.

REEF OS

Although coral reefs are thought to occupy only 0.1% of the planet, they are the nursery of at least 25% of all marine life. Nearly one billion people on earth depend on it for their food supply. Somewhere in a UN audit office, the annual global financial value of the ecosystem services of coral reefs such as coastal protection is estimated at 30 billion dollars, or 350,000 dollars per hectare. You can add another 36 billion if we add the income from tourism. The bad news is that coral reefs are under tremendous pressure. Due to a destructive cocktail of warming and acidification of the seawater, agricultural pesticides and fertilisers that find their way to the sea via rivers, irresponsible tourism and overfishing, coral reefs are dying out at a rapid rate.

If we do nothing, the curtain will finally fall on the most colourful and most biodiverse ecosystem that planetary history has ever known. And that's a shame not only because of the breathtakingly beautiful underwater cosmos that disappears as a result, but also because coral reefs still have a treasure

trove of secrets to reveal. Because as soon as we start looking at a coral reef as a control system, it is based on interesting principles that can be inspiring in the transition to a future-proof society.

THE SEVEN 'DESIGN PRINCIPLES' OF A CORAL REEF

1   **A coral reef runs on direct sunlight**
    The ecosystem relies on a continuous flow of energy from one level to another (plants, herbivores, carnivores, scavengers, etc.) right through the food pyramid. Energy and nutrients are exchanged by species through a complex food web, but at its base, a coral reef runs on direct sunlight.

2   **Waste is food**
    Waste from one organism is food for another organism. The materials cycle is closed. Nothing goes to waste on a coral reef.

3   **Local balance**
    Ecosystems strive for balance by organising their most critical and vital interactions such as reproduction, pollination, or predator-prey relationships as locally as possible. When a species disappears (e.g. due to an epidemic), the balance is restored locally. This local focus contributes to the health of the ecosystem.

4   **Autonomy thanks to connectedness**
    Ecosystems consist of complex networks and interactions between organisms such as symbiosis (cooperation), predation (eating and being eaten) and competition. Organisms have a high degree of autonomy, but ironically this is due to their connection with other organisms.

5   **Resilience through diversity**
    The more diverse the ecosystem, the greater the ability to quickly find a new balance, bounce back and recover after a disruption.

6   **Distributed**
    Natural ecosystems, unlike most human structures, do not exhibit a centralised, but a decentralised and even distributed organisation. No single element is in complete control. Decentralisation and

distributed variation contribute to nature's adaptive capacity and
reduce the negative impact in the event of disasters or diseases.

7   Effectiveness instead of efficiency
In an economic system, efficiency ensures the highest possible profit-
ability. An ecosystem thrives mainly thanks to its effectiveness.

To explain the difference between efficiency and effectiveness during
workshops and lectures, I like to refer to how we make love. Making love
efficiently is goal-oriented, fast, decent and predictable. Making love
effectively is chaotic, slow, mischievous and unpredictable. I always leave
it up to the audience to decide what they like best. It is important that
they sense and remember the difference. Efficiency thinking is interesting
for taking advantage of a world of scarcity. Effectiveness is interesting to
contribute to a world that flourishes in abundance.

HOW CAN WE ...

- Do you want to create an intense moment of wonder with the experience of nature so that people can give their work and life a different
  direction?
- Drawing inspiration from natural ecosystems such as a coral reef
  when we want to prepare our port of Antwerp for a circular future,
  for example?
- Designing with love for nature when we want to organise a new residential area as a nature-inclusive and living ecosystem instead of grey,
  stone and cold structures?
- Using nature as a design guide if we want to decentralise and democ-
  ratise our energy system?
- Do you want to work with the (micro)biological processes of algae,
  bacteria and fungi and thus develop new generations of biodegradable
  and renewable raw materials, fuels and plastics?

How can we embrace the rapid wave of new legislation on
sustainability as a world of ability, rather than a world of must?

"Should Europe determine how much wattage my vacuum cleaner can have?
Is that what citizens are waiting for, ladies and gentlemen? I don't think so!"

In 2014, Frans Timmermans, as then Minister of Foreign Affairs in the Netherlands, sneered about "absurd, patronising and paternalistic European regulations". But shortly afterwards, as the architect of the European *Green Deal*
and European Commissioner, he knew better. With the *European Ecodesign*
Directive of 2005, we saved an astronomical 1,000 Terawatt hours (tWh) or
3.6 Petajoules of energy in Europe alone between 2009 and 2020.

> *With rules on refrigerators, washing machines,*
> *vacuum cleaners and other household appliances,*
> *more than four times the annual production*
> *of the Belgian nuclear power plant of Doel*
> *has been eliminated.*

When it comes to trends and transformation, we like to marvel at hip, disruptive start-ups. But despite the fact that legislation is not that sexy, it should
not be a blind spot. Good laws show everyone where the bar is set and provide
the entire industry with a so-called *'level playing field'*. Many Japanese, Chinese and American manufacturers of household appliances have also started
to apply the European Ecodesign Directive outside Europe. By leading the way
with legislation, a small continent can show the whole world the way.
Legislation, it better get on your radar: in its fight against litter, France
accelerated the European *Single-Use Plastics Directive* into a national law. An
American fast-food giant quickly anticipated this by providing its more than
three hundred restaurants in France with reusable fast-food packaging and
the necessary washing installations. On a blue Monday, the management
of a Belgian bakery chain choked on its coffee. It must have been a painful
moment to be beaten by an American fast food giant with a sustainable packaging innovation. The bakery chain with a Belgian signature, sustainable and
artisanal reputation and 260 restaurants in the world, twelve of which are in
France, had not seen this coming.

The CSRD (Corporate Sustainability Reporting Directive), the European Emissions Trading System (EU ETS), The Circular Economy Action Plan, the Extended Producer Responsibility Act (EPR), ... Each and every one of these new legislative frameworks is waves of change with the intention of guiding society as a whole, not through a green spray box, but through a sustainable transformation.

The European Climate Law clearly shows that clear legislative frameworks are beneficial for the environment and consumers, but also provide producers with new perspectives. It will prohibit the car sector from selling petrol and diesel cars on the European market by 2035. This not only allows European countries to take a big bite out of their carbon budget. It produces healthier air, and frees the European car industry from its so-called *path dependence*: if we want a European car industry in the next twenty years, the best European engineers had better be called in to produce better and cheaper batteries, instead of stubbornly continuing to work on energy-efficient diesel engines. Legislation can have a mission-driven and guiding effect. Thanks to the European scale, European-made electric cars will hopefully also have a democratic price level.

*Do we also know for our organisation which new laws
are coming, and which ones are relevant to us?
With whom in our organisation should we do
the exercise to map out those laws?
What do they mean for us in the coming years?
And how do they form a new framework for innovation?*

ELECTRIC EXCAVATORS, COFFEE CUPS AND CIRCULAR HAIR SALONS

The six largest municipalities in the Dutch province of North Brabant, including Eindhoven, Tilburg and Breda, have the ambition to only tender emission-free road works and construction projects by 2030. Reason enough for the family contractor Van der Zanden to electrify its entire machinery. To meet the new standards, Van der Zanden is pioneering electric excavators, oversized site batteries and power hubs to provide street workers and construction workers with battery-electric big guns. The business park is equipped with solar panels to charge the batteries as much as possible with energy from our own harvest. Their motivation:

'Those who are inspired by new legislation earn first.'

———————

CONTRACTOR VAN DER ZANDEN

The reverse is also possible. As an entrepreneur, you can also inspire the government to adopt new legislation. Billie Cups did just that with its reusable cups. Together with a broad alliance of organisations that each play their part in the logistics of reusable cups, they made an entire edition of the summer city festival Gentse Feesten free of disposable cups: a precedent that has led to one of the most progressive laws on single-use plastics.

The CSRD, which from 2024 will require some 50,000 European companies to report on their impact on people and the climate in a calibrated manner, will also affect their suppliers and customers. Green Circle Salons is a platform that takes care of the environmental policy of hairdressers in the United States and Europe from A to Z. Cosmetic waste, collected hair, reusable packaging, water-efficient nozzles, etc. The beauty sector can be a lot more beautiful thanks to a programme that is responsible for the sustainable logistics and communication of a hairdresser's shop on a large scale.

Thanks to this certification programme for the many, often small-scale barbershops, L'Oréal, the French world leader in cosmetics and personal care products, is able to complete its circle when it comes to eco-design and climate. After all, a significant impact of their products is made in the barbershop or in people's bathrooms.

'What does the CSRD mean to us?
And what does it mean for our customers and suppliers?
What impact will their CSRD-driven course
changes have on us?
And how can we make collaboration pay off?'

THE EUROPEAN QUARTER AND THE COURT OF JUSTICE AS A BATTLEGROUND

During the summer of 2023, research showed that industrial livestock farming in Europe receives no less than 1,200 times more public funding than producers of plant-based meat substitutes. This is an intriguing paradox when we realise that conventional animal agriculture has a crushing carbon footprint, while the emerging sector of cellular agriculture has the potential to rewrite the rules of the game worldwide. The new bevy of *cleanmeat* pioneers could usher in an era in which our food chains are freed from animal suffering, pollution of our surface waters, massive deforestation in the South and disproportionate use of space. Organisations that embrace animal rights and climate-friendly, plant-based eating habits should therefore head to the European quarter with a stall full of vegan *bitterballen* (fried meat-based snack). In this way, they can creatively address the imbalance and perhaps make more impact than if they only focused on the lifestyle and eating habits of consumers.

Today, policy and legislation are increasingly the battleground of activist forces. Measures on climate change are increasingly being enforced in courtrooms. Research from the London School of Economics revealed that between 2017 and 2022 as many as 2,000 climate cases took place in the world. The Belgian climate case, with its 60,000 co-plaintiffs, including many business leaders, is also an international flagship. In the year 2021, the government in Germany was taken to court no less than 15 times. Another turning point occurred in 2018 when oil and gas giant Shell was forced to its knees by Friends of the Earth Netherlands.

Advocate General of the European Court of Justice Eleanor Sharpston was right when she stated that a fish cannot go to court. At the intersection of environmental law and climate justice, the legal emancipation of vulnerable ecosystems has become the fastest-growing legal movement today, according to Jessica den Outer in her book *Rights for Nature*. From the Whanganui River in New Zealand to the heavily polluted Mar Menor in Spain, ... When natural ecosystems become legal entities in the same way as people, governments and companies, they can also be protected much more easily and ecocide is easier to punish.

Can the Meuse have a say in waste discharges? And can 3M be sued by the Western Scheldt? In the Netherlands, meanwhile, there are calls to give the

North Sea and the Wadden Sea legal protection, and in Flanders, nature associations and scientists led by Hendrik Schoukens are also arguing for nature to be given rights. Meanwhile, natural ecosystems are said to be protected as legal entities in 36 countries.

AND NOW?

Legislation is a silent force of change. In the coming years, armies of consultants will emerge to guide companies by the hand through new, legislative frameworks such as the CSRD. The risk is that we will allow ourselves to be fatigued again by doing checklist sustainability far away in our office towers. For impact professionals, the opportunity is to be at the forefront. You do this by embracing imminent legislation as a moving forward-framework with which the rules of the game are rewritten.

HOW CAN WE ...

- How can we, as an organisation, ensure that imminent new legislation is on our radar?
- How can we let our innovations be inspired by new legal frameworks in order to be at the forefront?
- Or vice versa: how can we, as a pioneer, make a more sustainable future visible and tangible in order to inspire legislators to work with new standards?

'A fish can't go
to court.'

———

ELEANOR SHARPSTON,
ATTORNEY GENERAL
AT THE COURT OF JUSTICE OF THE EUROPEAN UNION

How do we use A.I. and other tools from the technology toolbox for positive, impactful purposes?

BRAINSTORMING WITH A MASTER FROM THE GOLDEN AGE

The seventeenth-century Netherlands was a period of artistic brilliance and social transformation. In the beating heart of the Golden Age of the Netherlands, one name stands tall in an artistic genre that would leave an indelible mark on art history: Peter Claesz (1597–1660), master of the still life.
While many of his colleagues at the time exhibited the opulence and decadence of their patrons in their still lifes, Claesz went his own way. His work rarely exhibited ludicrous displays of wealth. Instead, he focused on the simplicity of everyday objects. A peeled piece of fruit, a cracked walnut, a half-full glass of wine, a timepiece or extinguished candle, ... These modest items were central to his compositions in an economical light, pointing to the temporality and transience of life and were always an attempt to encourage people to humility and a godly lifestyle.

Artists at that time were not artisans, but alchemists of colour and meaning. The painter's tools and palette were limitless for that time. Their search for the perfect shades was in itself an adventurous journey around the world that grew bigger and bigger thanks to the rich supply from faraway places. From the dazzling vermilion extracted from mercury ore to the precious ultramarine from lapis lazuli mines in Afghanistan, ... The painters collected and honoured these treasures as precious stones. The recipes for the perfect linseed oil-based paint were well-kept family secrets. Their studios were laboratories of creativity, technology, and meaning in an era of change.

In the Rijksmuseum in Amsterdam, art historian guides still pay tribute every day to the mastery with which Pieter Claesz managed to immortalise the inside of, say, a curly lemon peel with razor-sharp detail.

In the scene of sliced shallots on the right, you could acknowledge the Master's hand. Nevertheless, there is not a single shallot in his entire oeuvre. But because I needed an image to depict the 'layering' of sustainability,

I thought it would be an amusing idea to brainstorm with a painter from the Golden Age.

If only because we can.

What is easy to interpret today thanks to our knowledge of Midjourney (a generative artificial intelligence tool that allows you to generate images based on clear descriptions), would only shortly before have been labelled as madness or magic.

Think back to the moment you would walk into a record store in 1998. If you had told the owner back then that a 'digital record store' was coming up where you could listen to almost the entire history of music via a copper wire, 24/7, anywhere in the world, for 10 euros a month or less ... He would also most likely have considered it madness or magic.

Although this book is still written in a very traditional way – writing line by line and deleting a lot – I also greedily used A.I. to make beautiful images together with illustrator Mieke Geenen, but also to brighten up my text where necessary every time fatigue tried to creep into my sentences.

'Any technology that is sufficiently advanced is indistinguishable from magic.'

———————

SIR ARTHUR CHARLES CLARKE, SCIENCE FICTION WRITER

DIGITAL IMPACT GENIUSES

The rapid rise of generative A.I. has prompted my colleagues Manu Vollens and Jan Leyssens to build their own GPT. Over the course of three half-days, they set up Impactgenie.ai where each organisation can generate its own long-term impact strategy on the basis of brief input. The strategic paths are neatly set out in a report with your sustainability challenges, your impact opportunities (neatly structured according to the SDGs) and a step-by-step roadmap with instructions on how to measure and communicate impact.

*'People are not good at understanding complexity.
Computers are, and sustainability issues are complex.'*

————————

JAN LEYSSENS, 'WE ARE IMPACT COLLECTIVE'

But Manu and Jan are certainly not the only ones. In the next box, you will find a series of existing initiatives in which exponential technology is used to make an impact. After all, a lot of 'unsustainability' is the result of an economy and society that took shape in the 19th and 20th centuries, but which no longer meets the challenges of the 21st century. And the power of digital is mainly to get things better organised.

THE DOOM AND GLOOM OF AI

Instead of worrying that AI will make us obsolete, we would be better off spending the time on getting to grips with how vital our capacity for reflection, critical thinking, and emotional intelligence is becoming. Because the prejudices and damage that AI is already spreading are an echo of existing imperfections.

The benefits affair that toppled the Dutch government (Rutte III, 2021) is often attributed to overly strict controls by overzealous civil servants. But at the root of that was an AI-based risk profiling system that wrongly flagged 1.4 million people as fraudulent due to bias. Tens of thousands of people were pushed into poverty and thousands of children were wrongly placed in foster care. How do we ensure that this never happens again, let alone that escalations occur on a much larger scale?

Ashyana-Jasmine Kachra, AI regulation and policy expert at OpenAI (the products of ChatGPT and Dall-E) is already advocating for an ethical framework, put together by experts that is overseen by real people at all times.

According to research by ABN-AMRO, since 2018, $793 million has been invested in generative AI with sustainability applications. Despite the fact that AI is a real energy gobbler, according to the scientific journal *Nature*, the potential would be positive on balance if AI is used to achieve positive impacts, such as better directing smart energy grids, supporting designers in material-efficient design, formulation of new, bio-based material types and monitoring the effects of climate change.

TECH FOR GOOD

- Let's start with 'Responsible AI'. Since 2020, London-based Holistic AI has been a pioneer in creating governance frameworks for AI within organisations and companies. This enables AI systems that are explainable, robust, unbiased, and not prone to privacy violations.
- The financial and economic newspaper De Tijd launched ESG-district, a chatbot that allows you to quickly get answers to your questions about the sustainability efforts of Belgian companies. ClimateChat does exactly the same to browse through the IPCC's voluminous climate reports with the comfort of questions and answers.
- PersefoniGPT, a Large Language Model that helps companies measure and report their emissions, is head and shoulders ahead in its genre on the capital market.
- Clarity A.I. is an all-round sparring partner for sustainability professionals who want to bring more social impact to the market.
- Wageningen University & Research is using AI to analyse bird flight patterns so that wind turbines in the Maasvlakte and the North Sea can be switched off in time to prevent accidents.
- Gale van Tomorrow.io is a chat assistant that uses satellite data to update companies in the agricultural and maritime sector on expected weather conditions and how to respond to prevent disasters or losses due to severe weather.
- RWI-Synthetics creates virtual replicas, or digital twins of cities, as a policy instrument to simulate the effects of climate change and sustainability interventions.
- There is no 'planet B', but in the meantime, the Austrian Blackshark.ai is working on a digital twin of the planet to unleash real-time data and predictions on climate.
- Will we soon be able to break down plastic, clean rivers, make bioplastics and arm crops against diseases thanks to synthetic proteins? The Dutch company Cradle is unleashing machine learning on the connections between protein structures and their functions in order to engineer new proteins. According to McKinsey, as many as 60% of our materials can be given new, biobased alternatives thanks to computational biology.

- With its AI chief Giuseppe, the Chilean company NotCo is developing endless combinations to come up with new formulations for meat and dairy substitutes with plant-based raw materials. The flavours are tested by Giuseppe himself by analysing the brain waves of test subjects.
- Singapore-based AI Palette extracts market trends from sales data in the food sector and makes its insights available to product developers to develop new food and beverage concepts.
- Augmenta is working on a cloud platform that will support more and more design functions in the construction industry to reduce waste and energy waste.

In such a list, it is particularly striking that we should not see AI so much as an omniscient oracle, but rather as a creative sparring partner: a powerful tool or new entity in our team with which we can be much more productive.

TALKING TO TREES AND ANIMALS

There must have been a moment when people knew how to control the fire, thought they could bring the gods to their knees with it, but ended up burning their fingers on it and mainly cooking their food with it. Fire, language, music, … From hand axes to mobile phones and bacteria that produce milk: a technology first exists as a wild, mythical or magical idea before it is created, applied, accepted, becomes operational, etc. And then quickly feels like something very natural. Very occasionally they become the symbol of a civilisational leap; often they also have a dark side.

I felt once again that AI also offers magical perspectives when Milan Meyberg won the Mark Cornelissen Brightland Award with his Emissary of GAIA. If you were to scatter hundreds of thousands of biodegradable helicopter seeds over the Amazon rainforest with microscopic sensors, you could measure and calculate the condition of such an immense nature reserve in real time, calculate it and have a conversation about it with Mother Nature in human language.

The Earth Species Project is *completely astounding*. Here, machine learning is used to analyse the often very complex vocal interaction of crows, pigs or dolphins, as well as the choreography of bees. The goal: to crack the language of animals in order to be able to understand animal language, and – who knows – to be able to talk to animals one day. If we can decipher the language of animals through technology, would it change our relationship to the animal kingdom?

HOW CAN WE ...

- How can we harness the power of exponential technology like generative AI to make a positive impact?
- How can we use technology to make visible what is invisible and give it much better social and ecological control?
- How can we give AI a place in our teams to use as a creative sparring partner on a daily basis?
- How can we use new technologies to create new social structures that make existing systems less self-evident?

6 THE POWER OF CREATIVE COLLABORATION

*How do we ensure that we move forward together
so smoothly that our conflicting views ultimately turn out
to be of little importance?*

ARM WRESTLING FOR THE BIG RIGHT

There are techno-optimists, climate modernists, and climate alarmists, but did you know that there are also energy maximalists (when we bet on endless energy thanks to nuclear fusion, for example, we can solve all problems)? And also climate urbanists (only compact urbanisation with climate-oriented, living structures will protect us from the climate shock and therefore deserves focus), limitarians (when there is a maximum of financial wealth, it leads to redistribution and social equality), eco-globalists (only thanks to regulation can we put an end to fossil fuels and destruction of our ecosystem) and even neopastoralists (we first head for disaster and then return towards a harmonious, agrarian lifestyle)?

Each and every one of them are frames, clichés, labels even... that puts committed people in a box. They may point to a possible tunnel vision, but they usually do not do justice to the full view that is needed on such complex and intertwined themes such as climate, (in)equality, democracy and technology.

HYPNAGOGIA

To prevent innovation projects from slipping into ideological talking points where participants arm wrestle for the big right, I always think of Thomas Edison (1847–931). Considering the number of patents to his name (from the light bulb to the forerunners of the record player and video camera), he qualifies for the title of 'greatest inventor ever'. He is said to have come up with his ideas by exposing himself to hallucinations several times a day. And you don't need magic mushrooms to do it. Between waking and sleeping, there is a dream state called hypnagogia. If you sit up in a chair and take daily naps with your creative challenge in mind and coins in your hand, they will fall to the floor when you fall asleep. You wake up, and you harvest ideas and images that are completely free from the inhibiting effect of your inner critic and your rational brain. A notebook at the ready and voila: you can get started as a dreamcatcher every day.

In my workshops I don't make people hallucinate, but I do try to lower their inner protest voice by a few decibels. Because being right has little value during a creative collaboration. What counts is moving forward together.

Instead of a contemplative and judgmental mental state, you need to get your entire group into an open, playful, collaborative creative mode. That's why I've long been a devout believer in Design Sprint. With Google Ventures in Silicon Valley as its birthplace, Design Sprint provides a process focused on speed, accumulation of focus and efficiency. In this methodology, a bizarre fatwa has been issued about 'brainstorming'. Brainstorming is seen as a creativity-destroying activity, which at best only produces consensus-oriented solutions, which are not always the best and most sustainable. Brainstorming is replaced by a tightly directed script of interconnected exercises. Sometimes these exercises take place in groups, but usually participants work out certain sub-tasks individually. A Sprint is characterised by the many moments when participants are focused on their work and you can enjoy a stoic silence. Ironically, if you make space for brainstorming, discussion, deliberation, and debate, you'll make leaps and bounds in your creative process much faster. After all, your entire process is freed from redundancy and disinfected from hierarchy, ego, clinging to old ideas and meeting culture.

The process starts with a strategic challenge and ends with a solution that has been tested with a small group of (potential) customers or users. You will work in a small, fixed group where participants have clear roles. You work together continuously for three, four or five days and you follow a standardised, result-oriented, practical, clear and measurable process.

FROM SYMPHONIC ORCHESTRA TO JAZZ MUSIC

But a Sprint often feels like a marathon. With Design Sprint you make leaps, but it requires a lot of commitment from your participants (five days!), a lot of discipline and energy. Today, my workshops are more like a jazz session where a game is played with unpredictability than a conductor chasing a string quartet through a score with a stick in hand.

During a Provotyping session, you construct a vision of the future in a team, but we also choose how we are going to make it visible and tangible, and how we are going to elicit as much engagement as possible.

Everything starts with creating a context where a group can focus its stream of thoughts, but at the same time allow it to meander freely. The desire to participate is triggered by the prospect that we are going to prescribe an attractive narrative for the future. However, the prerequisites for a successful provotyping session remain consistent with the general principles of Design Sprint and other forms of creative collaboration:

HOW CAN WE ...

- How can we create space for creative collaboration in our organisation?
- How can we structurally connect with other organisations, within and outside our sector?
- How can we create the creative culture in our organisation where innovation and experimentation are given the necessary space, not as an exceptional event, but as a method to move forward?

SEVEN SUCCESS FACTORS
OF CREATIVE COLLABORATION

1 **Focus**
You start from a razor-sharp formulated challenge that achieves a strategic impact goal for each party. This keeps everyone on the same page throughout the process.

2 **Time limit**
People perform at their best when they don't have enough time for it. It limits the scope for excessive perfectionism.

3 **Diversity**
Bring people from different backgrounds and skills to the table. By bringing together people from all links in the value chain, even far beyond the boundaries of your own sector, you guarantee the necessary range of perspectives.

4 **Inspiration**
Open windows and doors wide to let in inspiration from other sectors and knowledge domains.

5 **Multiple mindsets**
Practise strategic and analytical thinking, as well as creative, narrative, tactile (with the hands) and empathetic thinking. Balance divergent thinking (broad idea generation), with convergent thinking (selection and focus) In this way, you activate the innovative power of everyone, shine multiple lights on your challenge and make leaps.

6 **Prototyping**
Make your solutions visible and tangible as early as possible in the form of an intervention or experiment. Closely observe the interaction with your subjects and learn where you need to optimise your solution to increase the desired impact.

7 **Iteration**
Experiments must be thoroughly evaluated so that we can incorporate all the lessons learned in the next step and continue to experiment with the future with enthusiasm.

'Being right is of little value
during a creative collaboration.
What counts is moving forward together.'

THE POWER OF WELL-BEING IN THE WORKPLACE

A better world starts in the workplace.

When we talk about well-being in the workplace, you might think of yoga, breathing exercises, and burnout prevention. And although they make a big difference for many people, a conversation with Siviglia Berto about well-being will always start or end with the basics: do workers actually have access to drinking water? Are there also women's toilets on the long circum navigation? And do we know how employees with a migration background feel more at home in the workplace?

Siviglia Berto has more than 25 years of experience in supporting organisations around sustainability and well-being and is the no-nonsense feminist at the helm of the start-up B-Tonic within the Swiss Baloise Group. In addition, she is a passionate adventurer who organises expeditions and trips for entrepreneurs and teaches them to leave their comfort zone. As a half-Italian, she likes to go out in the Dolomites and Aosta valley. There, she soon notices that the road to the top is different for everyone, but that both start and end points are the same.

Siviglia grew up in the 'commune of Sint-Martens-Latem', where sustainability was taught at an early age. The commune was one of the pioneers in organic and vegetarian food that reached its peak in the period after May '68. In the middle of the forests of Sint-Martens-Latem, this connecting place of people from all over the world with ecological ideas was created. It quickly became one of the Belgian showpieces for the meeting between East and West. 'The commune' was known for its non-conformist ideas and as a pioneer in sustainability. The community was almost 100% self-sufficient.

This life experience shaped Siviglia into someone who resolutely opts for the best of both worlds. For more than 25 years, as an impact entrepreneur, she has been challenging other entrepreneurs to actually integrate sustainability and connect it to well-being. No radical activism as in the commune, but a pragmatic entrepreneurial spirit imbued with authenticity and creativity. The key to change lies in the right combination of elements: entrepreneurship, authenticity, resilience, creativity and a culture focused on sustainability and the people themselves. For example, she offers support to entrepreneurs, HR experts, prevention and sustainability managers in creating positive impact with her People Sustainability Tool. Together with Siviglia, concrete impact cases are developed for organisations, based on Provotyping workshops. We start by questioning and improving sustainability and well-being in the workplace. When we involve people in a reflection exercise on, say, drinking water in the workplace, and they can make a difference there, they will also be more motivated to think about the impact of their company on drinking water reserves elsewhere. At B-Tonic, we call this 'People Sustainability': we first work on the scale level of everyone's work and home situation and then look further and think bigger.

WHY MAKE WELL-BEING AT THE HEART OF A SUSTAINABLE BUSINESS MODEL?

"The search for an effective and sustainable well-being policy is not an easy exercise, taking into account different profiles and a great diversity within organisations. Until recently, it was generally assumed that well-being and the urge to perform were opposites," blogs British performance psychologist Fran Longstaff. Those who wanted to perform had to sacrifice well-being or vice versa. The way in which organisations manage performance and well-being (burnouts, resilience issues, work-life balance, etc.) as binary strategies are the best proof of that law. Today, that 'logic' is under attack more than ever. Employers, employees and stakeholders see well-being and profit as reinforcing, complementary forces. The real challenge lies in developing environments that encourage sustainable performance, with an eye for both results and well-being. However, it is still far from clear to everyone how that model fits in with an ESG (Environment, Social, Governance) strategy.

WELL-BEING WITH THE 'S' OF ESG

The mental health and well-being of employees must form the measurable basis of the 'S' or the social component within ESG. Well-being is the result of a number of levers that are applied in a consistent and organisation-wide way. So it's (much!) more than a strategy of words and the occasional small gesture like a yoga class, a piece of fruit or free coffee. The end goal is about the culture that an organisation and its leaders foster to make the work environment a powerful, fantastic place where employees are listened to and where they feel safe, valued, and trusted. Only when the well-being or 'S' reaches a healthy balance does the success rate of initiatives in the field of the 'E' and the 'G' also increase.

WHAT IS PEOPLE SUSTAINABILITY?

- The concept of People Sustainability combines employee well-being with sustainability undertake.
- In other words, at the intersection of these two aspects, a sustainable Welfare policy is born.
- By putting people at the heart of your organisation, you promote:
  » loyalty and making your employees feel good
  » the company's results
  » ESG Reporting

(Today, more and more organisations base their policies on ESG criteria. They are trying to reinvent and improve themselves in a world where social and environmental needs are increasingly prioritised and where sustainability has become the key to (business) transformation.)

With a People Sustainability approach in which people are central, organisations and companies are more resilient, capable of more, more innovative and more motivated to achieve the joint sustainability goals. That new understanding was high on the agenda of the World Economic Forum 2023 and is defined as treating people within an organisation ethically and fairly.

6 PILLARS OF PEOPLE SUSTAINABILITY

People Sustainability gives six important, irreplaceable qualities to a company:
1 Diversity, Equity, and Inclusion (DE&I)
2 Well-being and balance
3 Trust and transparency
4 Health and Safety
5 Empowerment and growth
6 Societal objective

THIS IS HOW THE MAGIC WORKS

People Sustainability can only work its magic if you, as an organisation, have an eye for each of these four domains:

1 **Sociological**
Management should create work environments where everyone feels welcome and is actively involved. So, diversity and inclusion are an advantage and a strength.

2 **Psychological**
The mental well-being of employees is important. They should be able to work in a healthy and supportive environment that not only provides security but also fosters their loyalty, productivity, and personal development.

3 **Environment**
Social and environmental sustainability go hand in hand. A talent programme, too. Also known as green HR management, it is being developed to attract people who are environmentally conscious. This programme includes training and ensures that sustainability becomes an integral part of the daily reality of the employees.

4 **Strategy**
Part of the sustainability strategy is building a talent roadmap. This helps organisations to find the right people or partnerships, which is worth its weight in gold for their employer branding.

POWERFUL INVESTMENT WITH SUSTAINABLE IMPACT

Sustainable entrepreneurship has become an important aspiration of employees looking for meaning for their professional ambitions linked to job choice. This is both to attract new talent and to connect current employees. In fact, research by consultant Deloitte shows that 68% of employees and 81% of top management prefer better well-being to moving up the career ladder. In other words, behind the front line of the current 'war for talent', there has been a real 'war for well-being' for several years now. An HP study of more than 15,000 knowledge workers in 12 countries shows that 83% of those employees are willing to earn less with an employer that values factors for happiness at work, such as emotional intelligence, trust and freedom of choice. The UK's Bupa Wellbeing Index comes to the same conclusion: employees will accept a 19% salary cut if they can work for an ethically responsible or environmentally friendly organisation. That percentage rises to 23% for Generation Z, which makes up an increasing share of the workforce.

The classic approach to employment relationships is an old psychological contract. There, the employer is a stable 'caring' employer with loyal employees in the permanent core of the organisation. The 'dark side' here is that employees experience a golden, comfortable cage as demotivating. In today's philosophy, the employee assumes an employment relationship based on mutual fit, which can also be temporary. The employer sees itself more as a flexible employer with a fixed core, but also a flexible pool. As a result, employees gain flexibility and freedom. They are freed from the golden cage, but unfortunately they also risk uncertainty. They feel detached and can't find a connection.

MAGIC & DARK SIDES

Peggy De Prins, professor of (sustainable) HRM/Academic Director of the Masters in Strategic HRM at Antwerp Management School, points to the negative impact of the 'dark sides', such as stress and work pressure, on employee retention and attracting the talent of tomorrow. 'Employees leave if they have to keep too many things under the radar. This is a great pity, especially in the context of the 'war for talent'. We need to invest in continuous listening,' says Peggy De Prins.

She continues: "It starts with discussing the real issues or 'dark sides'. There you magically find out what is really going on within an organisation and what is taboo and what is not. Continue to build an open culture and ensure that employees always feel safe without having to go through an internal person. Engage an external party that can channel this much better. In this way, you find out where stress and pain points arise and which interventions you can use to act."

+1 THE POWER OF INVESTING

Today's money determines tomorrow's world.

This piece is a guest post by Astrid Leyssens. As a sounding board, Astrid sheds light on the investment policy of family offices, impact funds, and the strategy of impact start-ups. In addition, she shares her expertise internationally with great generosity through guest lectures at universities. She has a particular interest in the transformation of our food system, the transfer of capital from one generation to the next and the transition to a more inclusive and socially just society. I got to know Astrid when I worked as a strategic planner in the advertising sector and Astrid was Marketing Director at a well-known producer of ecological cleaning products. Since then, we have continued to follow each other's careers. In this text, Astrid takes us to the world of 'money', and how you can create impact with it.

WITH IMPACT INVESTMENT, YOU ARE MAINLY BUILDING BRIDGES

In recent years, my fascination with the financing journey of impact start-ups has led to a methodical approach with which I bridge the gap between impact start-ups, impact funds and large capital providers. I notice that I achieve an acceleration when actors in those three worlds can work together more efficiently. Another lever that gives me a lot of satisfaction is teaching next-gen high-net-worth individuals. After my lectures, many of the next genners in Argentina, Switzerland, the US, Belgium and the Netherlands are already working with impact funds, philanthropy, have started to look differently at wealth tax, or are building their own portfolio with impact ventures. It is so that I can contribute something with my talent to turn the tide. When that succeeds, it gives a lot of satisfaction.

WE ARE IMPACT COLLECTIVE

Connection is something that often comes back in my work. Fortunately, the number of people who want to use my career for an attractive future is growing rapidly. For example, in 2022 research agency Edelman had already measured that 7 out of 10 people among employees also want a job with a meaningful goal as motivation. An average career has 90,000 active hours, and perhaps the most impactful decision you can make in your life is how you're going to spend that valuable time. The biggest source of waste is the waste of talent, the Dutch historian Rutger Bregman would say, and for me he is 100% right. To give Impact Professionals shelter and a professional network, I founded 'We Are Impact Collective' in 2023, which Stefaan Vandist also joined as a club member from the very beginning. Impact-driven leadership, innovation, storytelling, finance, … Everyone has their own focus, clients and expertise, but as an alliance we work together on projects with scale that we might not easily get to as individuals. Think of the development of a creative incubator that also serves as an Impact Exhibition Space, or 'generosity days' where we collectively help start-ups and non-profits move forward.

With We Are Impact Collective, I also want a group of experts from diverse backgrounds to work together to:
- bring more investment money to impact funds and impact ventures more quickly
- make organisations more inclusive and nature-restorative
- develop business models that are regenerative
- accelerate the principle of giving money
- and to question current economic models based on power, position and control.

IMPACT INVESTING AS LEVERAGE

Impact investing is the investment of capital in organisations that want to solve a specific social or environmental problem with a company or fund. The difference with donating is that a business logic is used. In other words, a solution is devised that rotates in the gearbox of the economy in order to achieve financial added value, but also social or ecological gains. Entrepreneurship is the driving force, design is the navigation map and ethics is the compass, as Jan Leyssens, colleague at We Are Impact Collective, would put it. An impact investor provides fuel and selects investments based on a number of criteria such as:

1 What does the organisation want to solve?
2 Who is it a solution for?
3 And how long does it take to achieve the desired impact?

The challenges that can conquer your heart are very diverse:

With too much CO_2 in the atmosphere, investing in clean tech solutions or nature-based solutions that capture and store carbon are an option. If there is too little homework help available for children from vulnerable families, you can invest in an organisation that offers an accessible and affordable service. There are 1,001 social and environmental challenges where solutions are queuing up to get financial oxygen.

Some of these solutions are already well financed and the investment market for these solutions is already mature, for example in the financing of solar energy or battery technology for electric cars.

Many impact investors therefore attach great importance to how 'additional' their investment is: today, you may make a bigger difference per euro if you invest in the development of plant-based meat substitutes for the American market, regenerative agriculture in India, STEM education in Central Africa, etc. than when you invest in Scandinavian wind turbines.

In the case of impact investments, too, there are so-called *asset classes*: investment categories that say something about the spread over different forms of capital. For example, a listed stock is a different type of asset than a loan or direct investment in a company. Most impact investors who build a portfolio will ask themselves a number of questions: What social or environmental issue is close to our hearts? Which challenge is so urgent? Which solution is the most effective? Or most unsurpassed? How much risk can be borne? And how do I ensure that these principles are translated into all my asset classes?

If '(underprivileged) poverty with us' is close to your heart, you can invest in social housing as well as in the range of affordable subscription formulas for green energy solutions.

Impact investing requires a lot of homework. A lot of time is often spent getting to know and assessing the teams behind Impact Organisations that bring ideas to fruition. Impact investment is about both financial and social returns, and that involves twice as many considerations.

WHAT CAN WE EXPECT IN THE COMING YEARS?

The capital invested in impact investments has been growing steadily in recent years. I see more and more newcomers among impact funds, impact start-ups and impact investors. You feel that what was once special is becoming more and more normal as more and more traditional banks, funds, private investors and pension funds jump on the bandwagon.

This growth is due to the increased visibility of urgencies, as well as the growing range of impact investing opportunities and their outcomes. Another explanation is that more and more capital is finding its way to the younger generations. And because more and more women are at the helm, different criteria are used in value creation. In addition, you also see legislative frameworks increasingly moving in a sustainable direction. The ecosystem of the initial pioneers is now surrounded by impact communities, knowledge institutes, experts and research partners who are enabling a mental shift.

More and more experienced impact investors have selected themes that give them a personal mission and that they also delve into in terms of content. They create thematic portfolios of philanthropic and investment solutions. Sometimes it also goes further by placing the themes high on the agenda in companies where they have a mandate. It is often referred to as shareholder activism: placing themes such as human rights or biodiversity high on the agenda of the board or shareholders' meeting and critically examining one's own board culture and composition.

TRANSITION FINANCING

There is no such thing as a struggle with only one theme, because we do not live lives with only one theme, according to the famous feminist Audre Lorde in her 1982 speech on the Civil Rights Movement in America. Indeed, societal challenges are not isolated. They are intertwined and entangled in what we often call 'the polycrisis' today.

A growing group of impact players therefore wants to take their engagement to a higher level. Many challenges are so complex and systemic in nature that the classic problem-solving approach threatens to oversimplify the context and often leads to symptom relief in a well-intentioned manner. Systemic Impact or Transition Finance uses new principles such as:

- Investigating and uncovering underlying, systemic interconnections.
- Shaping partnerships between players with complementary expertise before funding them.
- Setting up more *'distributive governance models'* where nature or disadvantaged groups are given a louder voice in the boardroom, technology such as AI can lead to better decisions, or where simply more women are represented.

As a result, impact investors who are committed to helping the homeless, for example, will invest in both immediate needs, such as more beds during the winter, and in indirect solutions, such as the availability of mental health care for vulnerable young people. The various systemic layers of social problems will therefore also be visible in their portfolios.

Because systemic investors use the systemic map of a challenge, they are not limited by specific industries. Place-based impact investing looks with a similar wide-angle lens where different people, organisations, networks, and capital are pooled to solve problems in a particular place. The work to set up collaboration is still in the phase of creating blueprints, as it was in the beginning of the circular economy. Only in recent years have we learned about the root causes of numerous social and environmental problems, and today we are making the switch from impact KPIs to more systemic metrics. We start by focusing on a desired end result and map out an iterative path to get there.

Impact investing can act as a driver of change. It is important that we continue to take a critical look at ourselves. How should we deal with the increasing concentration of wealth in successful impact investments in a time of growing inequality? Is it acceptable for there to be a surplus of money among a certain group in society, while many are lacking? Isn't the government better suited to tackle societal and environmental challenges than start-ups that have to navigate funding rounds? And isn't the foundation of our economic system, without an upper limit, at the root of the many problems that need to be solved? And how can we expect a small, privileged group to solve contemporary problems?

A NEW ECONOMIC MODEL

Various new economic models seek to provide a more structural response to the root causes of these problems. Well-known examples, such as Kate Raworth with the Doughnut Economy, as well as the Purpose Foundation's recipes in which economics serves society instead of the other way around, and the new ownership model Steward Ownership, are models that seek economic solutions at the grassroots. Degrowth is also one that fits in the current list. You don't change the world by fighting the system, but by building a new system, which makes the old system obsolete. This is a famous quip about system change by Richard Buckminster Fuller.

Shareholder capitalism seems to be the only model that can underpin the economy, but from a historical perspective its dominance and self-evidence is still relatively recent. What economic model do we have in front of us? Much is sustained by identity. As a successful entrepreneur, your entire self-image is based on being successful as an entrepreneur and being wealthy as a self-made (wo)man. Who are you with that worldview if you don't manage to achieve even more financial success every year? There is a need for in-depth reflection and inner development goals to make this transition possible. What if the game isn't about the capital gains you realise, but about how much you leave behind? What if we don't optimise for ownership, but for constructive contribution and legacy?

The impact investor who focuses on transition realises that investments in system innovation are the real solutions. Bringing together groups of people from all walks of life who want to steer a different course, and encouraging each other to take the necessary steps in times of necessary transition, is crucial. Some think that there are almost enough people with a new worldview to tip the system, others think that we are already past that. In any case, it is a courageous adventure to contribute to with the best of ourselves. In the growing polycrisis, we will have to steadfastly maintain this course in increasingly difficult circumstances. In doing so, we will have to continue to work on places of hope that give cooperation a home and where the challenges can be looked straight in the eye with the necessary pleasure from different disciplines.

'I've never done it before,
so I think I can.'

———

2
WHAT IF

___

The seed of everything lies in the unfolding of an attractive and connecting vision of the future. A stimulating look at the future is more powerful than numbers and statistics. It offers a dot on the horizon and puts our motives under the right tension. With a guiding vision of the future, the narrative of your organisation or initiative can take shape step by step.

GILBERT'S NUCLEAR ENERGY LAB

What if your daughter or son gave you a nuclear reactor as a birthday present? That sounds bizarre, but in 1951 it wasn't so bad.

INCLUDING ~~BATTERIES~~ URANIUM

The Gilbert Atomic Energy Lab is the brainchild of *Alfred Carlton Gilbert*: athlete, inventor, magician, entrepreneur and the largest toy manufacturer of its time. With a real *cloud chamber*, young people could work radiantly and feverishly with low-level radioactive material in order to accelerate particles up to 20,000 kilometres per second. For those who have seen the film *Oppenheimer* (2023), Gilbert wrote the manual together with General Leslie Groves, the director of the Manhattan Project (the development of the atomic bomb). Retail price of the toy: $49.00. Converted, that would be about $600 today.

Although the game box has often been called one of the most irresponsible toys of all time, Gilbert has always maintained that it was "perfectly" safe. As long as you follow the rules carefully, your exposure to radiation is never greater than during a day of sunbathing on the beach. In addition to being an inventor and businessman, Alfred Carlton Gilbert was also an American patriot. He denounced the education system of the time because it would only produce "obedient sheep for offices and factories". With his A.C. Gilbert Company, he has conceived and marketed hundreds of different toy products. The source of his exceptional creativity was patriotism: "To maintain its lead over the rest of the world, the United States had to become a nation of scientists and engineers," he was convinced. Thanks to Gilbert, my parents' generation played with the first Meccano boxes, electric trains, remote-controlled boats, were the first young people to look through a microscope, or were given an educational discovery box full of scientific experiments under the Christmas tree.

YESTERDAY'S FUTURE

In his autobiography we read that the U.S. government supported the sale of his Atomic Energy Lab because it was a powerful propaganda tool to prepare the population for the imminent atomic age: a new era where abundant energy would provide limitless possibilities. Popular culture in the years that followed was full of visions of the future where children were picked up from school by flying cars, supersonic planes that took us to the other side of the world, or where vacations on Mars were spent in dome-shaped biospheres. Retro-futurism makes us feast on the imagination of the past. It gives us a glimpse into yesterday's future. Moreover, we can learn a lot from it:

- Visions of the future reveal the technological expectations and societal aspirations of a period, but also often reveal design trends, industry trends, aesthetic preferences, and the political context.
- Some futuristic images serve as social criticism. Artists and designers use visions of the future to respond to contemporary issues, challenge societal norms or seduce the public with alternative futures. Studying these critiques offers insight into the counterculture.
- Like The Atomic Energy Lab, retro-futuristic artifacts also often display educational purposes in schools and science centres. What were the educational intentions at the time? What does that say about the view of man and the world at the time? And how different or strange is our worldview today?

- A nice historical observation is that we almost always underestimate the speed of technological developments, but almost always overestimate the pace and adoption capacity of institutions and society. Just think of the self-driving car, cultured meat and genetic engineering.

A vision of the future always says much more about the time in which it was conceived than about the time it tries to portray.

When we dig deeper into history, we also learn that our desires and expectations for the future show a high degree of similarity over time. Since ancient times, we have dreamed of eternal youth, access to all the world's knowledge, the ability to fly like a bird, mind reading, world peace, even control over the weather and climate.

And perhaps that's why visions of the future are powerful tools. They offer us a dot on the horizon and show us which solutions we can believe in to fulfil timeless desires. In this chapter, we see why a vision of the future functions as the crankshaft that keeps your organisation strategically running, and how we can develop an inspiring and connecting vision of the future together.

PROVOTYPING
STEP 1
—
WHAT IF

STARTING WITH THE END

How would you describe the challenge of the future?

There are as many visions of the future as there are people, so certainly also in your team. When you use the Provotyping Canvas to start a process to write your future story, make it visible and tangible, it is best to start at the end. For example, by asking these types of questions:

- What challenge must we face in order to become an immortal organisation?
- What is the biggest challenge for people to be able to enjoy … (our products, chocolate, our city, mobility, etc.) ?
- Or much simpler: what is the future challenge for you that you want to face today?

Don't worry. This is a warm-up exercise that puts everyone in a creative and future-exploring group mode, while also getting used to the principles of the process. Each participant may write a challenge on a sticky note or even give a challenge to several sticky notes. No texts! Write them to legibly, and aim for a maximum of seven words per sticky note. As a moderator, it's your job to keep people working. You will see that this exercise gives a good idea of the beliefs that live in the group. In addition, they are also an ideal warm-up for the entire Provotyping exercise. Because Provotyping does not mean that we are going to waste time on endless debates or useless, unstructured discussions. Being right has little value in this process. What counts is getting ahead. It doesn't matter who wrote down exactly what. All statements on sticky notes are everyone's work material.

THE DECISION TREE

Exercise 1: The Decision Tree (Group Leader Instructions)

By creating a decision tree, you can create a group consensus from 10, 20 or more challenges in a short period of time.

1 Give the group three or four minutes to formulate some challenges individually. That can be anything! Internal challenges, market challenges, etc. legal, technical, organisational, reputational challenges, macroeconomic challenges, transition challenges, etc.

2 Have everyone briefly – 30 seconds – explain their challenges verbally to the group.

3 Stick all the sticky notes visibly together while naming them one by one.

4 Stick sticky notes on top of each other with basically the same thing written on top of each other.

5 Let participants – in silence! – cast three votes on the challenges that seem most relevant to him or her. This can be done with sticky colour dots or by placing dots with a coloured marker. Rules of the game: you can spread all three however you want. So you can give all three to the same challenge, shamelessly vote for your own challenges three times, or give a voice to three of the challenges you think are most relevant, ...

6 Then you stick the one or more sticky notes with the most votes at the top, then the sticky notes with the next number of votes below them, and so on ... Sticky notes that didn't get a vote are stuck next to each other on the bottom row.

7 The end result often resembles a Christmas tree... hence the word decision tree. The challenges that the group believes are most relevant are at the top, and those that are least relevant are at the bottom.

The decision-maker

During a provotyping process, one person is appointed as the decision-maker. Participants have to get used to that too. Provotyping is a workshop without democracy. He or she is the one whose task is to hear everyone, to oversee everything and to make the decision every time a decision has to be made. Participants can also get used to this during this warm-up exercise. The Provotyping canvas provides space at the top to stick the 'winning' challenge and its successors side by side.

THE DOMINANT REGIME

*What is the most common way
in which society fulfils a need today?*

Despite the fact that the world is subject to change, there is always a demonstrable 'dominant regime'. The dominant regime describes the existing
system, established practice, rules and norms that characterise the current
situation. To gain insight into the dynamics of change, we need an unambig-
uous picture of the present. Because the present is complex, we describe the
common way in which a position is filled or a problem in society is solved.

A good example can be found in driving. Despite the great social pressure
and the emerging alternatives such as car-sharing systems, ridesharing and
self-driving cars, car ownership is the most common (and for most people
the only self-evident) way to provide (car) mobility. You could describe the
dominant regime as 'in order to enjoy (car) mobility, I (or my employer) have
to buy a car and as a driver I bear the responsibility for it. Or you can describe
it in one word: car ownership'.

Is there any debate about how exactly you would describe the dominant regime?
Briefly hear each other's motivations, involve everyone in writing down varia-
tions, make a new decision tree and leave the choice to the decision-maker.

THE NEWCOMERS

Who are the inspiring newcomers ushering in change?

Now that we have defined the dominant regime of our sector, we can create a
collection of organisations, companies, politicians, entrepreneurs, researchers, activists, scientists, ..., artists, ... that undermine the status quo with new
solutions, new views, new organisational models and revenue models. So
we are looking for the *new-kids-on-the-block* who will disrupt the dominant
regime from below with a better alternative. Hereafter you will find a series
of examples of newcomers to the food sector. They show how, as a source of
inspiration, they breathe life and fuel into the creative process around a '*singularity supermarket*' and reveal new ways of thinking.

Therefore, instruct your team to create a presentation with some 'shining examples' that give a glimpse into new ways in which needs or functions are fulfilled. Or feed your creative process yourself with a presentation of unlikely, but existing, disruptive, transformative innovation examples to provide the necessary broadening of your horizons. Make sure your team can add at least five inspiring newcomers to their Provotyping canvas with conviction on a sticky note.

FORCES OF CHANGE

What are the five key forces of change impacting our industry?

Forces of change are broad waves of change that are crashing into society from the world of technology, law, geopolitics, shifts in socio-demography, ecology, culture, ... Others describe it as social pressure that the dominant regime has to endure. External forces of change are also referred to as *autonomous developments*: the large, global, social changes – or megatrends – to which you as an organisation can eagerly respond, but on which you can exercise little steering power.

Forces of change in the world of automobility are, for example: increasing climate awareness, the increased attention to the effect of air quality on health, the increased attention to safety and well-being, but also that new European climate law that bans cars with petrol or diesel engines by 2035, the switch to battery-electric cars and (who knows) hydrogen, the enormous capacity development to build new cars in China, the increasingly autonomous driving cars, the increasingly later age at which young people get a driver's licence, the ageing of car drivers, but certainly also the increasing traffic jams, despite the fact that we work from home more, ...

Ask all participants to individually fill in sticky notes with one change at a time. Let them write as many as they want and then, in dialogue with their neighbour, pick out the five most important ones.

Through the process of the decision tree, you can come up with a list of the five most relevant forces of change.

DEEPENING

Climate change, digitalisation, an ageing population, etc. To avoid too often the same, slightly too general autonomous developments on the table, you can always find inspiration from the better suppliers of future literature such as the German Zukunftsinstitut, Farsight from Copenhagen (society-wide), the London-based Future Laboratory (brands and marketing), Futurism (science and technology), Change.inc and Forum for the future (sustainability challenges), and so on... who always report with a fresh perspective on broad, social changes.

Transformation Maps on the World Economic Forum website is a tool that allows you to uncover connections between global challenges and global forces of change through powerful visualisations. Many institutes for the future offer handy card sets that document forces of change, such as the *Foresight Cards* of the Dutch IVTO. To get much closer to the future, you can also come up with fictional, but very realistic headlines to help your participants question the future.

Is it still difficult to come up with a top five in the multitude of changes? Organise them in a matrix consisting of two axes: Impact and Probability, and involve them not in your sector, but in your organisation. The changes in the quadrant with highest probability and highest impact deserve the most attention.

IMPACT

PROBABILITY

CRITICAL UNCERTAINTIES

Which critical uncertainties are most decisive for our future?

The top five forces of change already suggest a high probability of how that world of change can shape the future, but there are still considerable critical uncertainties.

There is no doubt that the aforementioned forces of change will completely transform the automotive industry. But in this transformation, will the car remain an individual entity? Or will the new generations of vehicles, infrastructure and organisational systems make efficiency gains by organising the mobility of people and goods more and more collectively?

Another issue that qualifies as critical uncertainty is society's ability to adapt. Just think of the energy transition in the automotive industry, the delaying political polarisation, the necessary charging infrastructure, energy supply, legislation on automation of mobility, affordability, etc. Will government agencies, legislators, and critical infrastructure providers be able to handle the speed of change? Or will so-called SRL (so-called Society Readiness levels) continue to lag behind TRL (Technology Readiness Levels)?

Determine with your team which are the two most critical uncertainties.

DEEPENING FUTURE SCENARIOS

When you have two critical uncertainties, you can turn them into a matrix figure again:
1   Individual versus collective: Will the car remain the symbol of individual freedom? Or will we, as a society, increasingly organise the mobility of goods and people collectively?
2   Will we, as a society, embrace the rapid pace of breakthroughs in technology and energy transition for the automotive industry? Or will the adaptive capacity of society, legislators and infrastructure builders slow down?

This results in four different worlds, or scenarios. In the world of strategic thinking about the future, scenario thinking is considered by many to be the most powerful, most used and most comprehensive tool. Martin Raymond, co-founder of London's renowned *Future Laboratory*, calls it '*the multiple futures machine*'. Where trend watching is aimed at identifying and interpreting significant (behavioural) changes or discovering and framing *the next big thing* as a marketing opportunity, future-exploring scenarios are descriptions of how the new can affect the lives of all of us.

Screenplays are essentially nothing more than fictional stories about possible futures that you've written inspired by forces of change, critical uncertainties, and observations on the front lines of innovation and counterculture. We are not only talking about the desirable future, but also the possible, probable, plausible, avoidable and, if possible, the almost unthinkable future. So they never lay claim to the future and are therefore not attempts at prediction. Rather, scenarios aim to broaden our horizons and loosen our collective thinking from the here-and-now mentality.

The exercise helps us better prepare for the future, however it unfolds. It is are there to provoke our existing, often limited ideas and want to surprise us with where the waves of change can take us. The most common methodology yields four visions of the future. It provides designers, marketers, executives or policymakers with in-depth insight and a common frame of reference. Ultimately, they help us to ask better leadership questions and identify what is worth pursuing and what should be avoided. Or as scenario planner and future explorer Kees van der Heijden puts it: scenarios are invitations to strategic debate.

CHARACTERISTICS OF
A SUCCESSFUL SCENARIO EXERCISE

When writing future scenarios, you can let your imagination run wild.
Some characteristics of a successful scenario exercise, as I like to see
them myself:

- Future scenarios are like movies. You know it's fiction, but with a
  believable setting, a noble fight against evil and an exciting plot, you'll
  stay captivated. A little sense of spectacle helps people to grasp the
  true impact.
- Successful future scenarios are layered future scenarios. One may be
  more desirable than the other, but a vision of the future should be full
  of contradictions, anomalies and shortcomings. That's what the world
  looks like today. Scenario thinking is not wishful thinking.
- Because most scenario exercises have a horizon of ten to thirty years
  ahead of them, there is plenty of room for change, but many elements are still easily recognisable. It is inevitable that you will find
  elements in your stories that are in fact already developing today.
  Recognisability is good so that people can find themselves in the
  story. The fact that we occasionally extend developments from the
  present to the future in a linear way is not necessarily a problem, as
  long as we are not blind to possible systemic shifts that lie ahead.
- Pushing the boundaries of decency is a good idea. A good screen-
  play has uncomfortable and even provocative elements. It forces us
  to question ourselves and the right of our organisation to exist, and
  that makes the debates that follow much more interesting. After all,
  choices have to be made.
- Scenarios don't have to be too long and don't have to explain
  everything in detail. Suggestion, a lack of meaning and open ends
  work well narratively. Movie trailers are almost entirely meaning-de-
  ficient, but they do sharpen your attention. They invite readers to
  connect with the further outcome and to fill in the existing white
  space with their imagination.

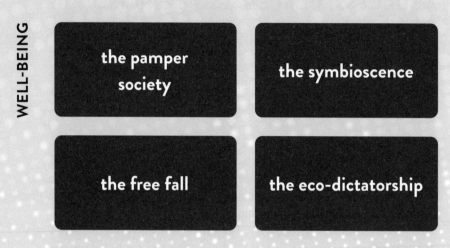

WELL-BEING

| the pamper society | the symbioscence |
| the free fall | the eco-dictatorship |

CLIMATE

For my book *Pretopia* (Lannoo Campus 2022, only published in Dutch),
I experimented with critical uncertainties for a while to write four exciting
short stories that bring different futures in my own city of Antwerp to life.
I set to work with the following critical uncertainties:

1   Will we, as an international community, be able to get climate change
    under control, or will it go completely out of control?
2   Will we still judge the success of society by Gross National Product,
    or will we create all kinds of additional metrics to measure increased
    quality of life and not just prosperity?

ANTWERP 2052

The eco-dictatorship, the pamper society, the free fall and the symbioscence are four stories about life in Antwerp, the state of the economy, the port of Antwerp and its relationship to the rest of the world and the climate. Those critical uncertainties lead to four completely different future scenarios, as the shortened versions below, show.

THE PAMPER SOCIETY
Despite the global ecological decline, most people enjoy a life that is as good or bad as ever. After the corona outbreak, an obsession with health puts the climate crisis in the background. Above all, technology serves convenience and well-being. Every company is concerned with well-being. Precision narcotics are on the daily menu. Antwerp's offices are becoming cyber farms, while the city is adapting to rising water levels. But doubts are rising about the viability of our contemporary world, and the call for a renewed contact with nature is growing stronger.

THE ECO-DICTATORSHIP
In 2052, the 'eco-dictatorship' dominates. After overcoming a series of health crises, the world has been hit by climate disasters and ecological implosions. Major economies, led by China, India and the US, are taking drastic measures and putting the UN in the shade. Mega-cities are densifying, while the countryside is becoming wild. Carbon quotas, limited space, and social inequality characterise life. Antwerp suffers as a laggard of the green economy with an Antwerp port that has become an industrial mausoleum and a stain on illegal trade. But a Humanist Spring is dawning with young people taking to the streets for a 'people-first' policy.

THE FREE FALL
Global scarcity due to climate change leads to food shortages, political instability and extremely weak governments. Natural resources have been privatised, the middle class thinned out. Antwerp has smog domes for the elite, while others are left to their fate to capricious circumstances. The remaining tropical rainforests are being bought up by e-commerce giants. Space exploration is the new obsession to distract the gaze. The Bulgarian artists' collective hacks Space One's Orbital Display, and parodies messages from the fake news era for millions of Flemish people. Social criticism adorns the night sky.

THE SYMBIOSCENCE

The anthropocene marked humans as a destructive force, but the symbio-ceen embraces a regenerative world in which humans, technology and nature merge. Climate change led to a collective consciousness and innovations in the chemical sector. The Port of Antwerp is flourishing as a hub for regener-ative technologies and is celebrating the tenth anniversary of the Declara-tion of Interdependence. Nature now has legal rights, and worldwide efforts are being made to promote the circular economy and interdisciplinary ecology in education. Decentralised platforms encourage contributions to regenerative solutions. The future is tied to a thriving planet.

THE DOT ON THE HORIZON

What is our long-term vision for the future?

Now that the group has an overview of forces of change, a dominant regime that is ready for something new, inspiring newcomers, critical uncertainties and possibly also some challenging future scenarios, we should be able to formulate a point on the horizon.

What we need now is a perspective that we as a team, but later also our employees, suppliers, customers and policymakers can fall in love with. The power of a question that starts with the words 'what if' is that your imagination is invited to answer that question with a new perspective. Provide a perspective that is not only attractive and appealing, but also sounds refreshingly new. Once again, you can work together and separately at the same time thanks to the decision tree.

- What if there was a new military service for the young generation to fight against the effects of climate change?
- What if you used artificial intelligence to distribute energy, raw materials and food equitably across the world?
- What if countries that focus on Gross National Happiness and Gross Ecological Product are better off than countries that don't?
- What if the materials you use to make your products today were banned tomorrow?
- What if, thanks to technology, we could talk to nature?
- But also: what if Rosa Parks couldn't get on the bus because of facial recognition technology?

Rephrase your sentence by replacing the beginning with 'what if' with 'we believe that', ... And hopefully you have a beautiful, innovative and appealing vision of the future that inspires your organisation and others to participate.

NINE INSPIRING PRACTICAL EXAMPLES OF CREATIVELY WORKED OUT VISIONS OF THE FUTURE

THOMAS D'HOOGE | FUTURE MUSEUMS IN THE METAVERSE

*What if future education were the basis
for creative education?*

Flanders' most passionate advocate for more future literacy in the social debate, Thomas D'hooge, is convinced that we should start at school. For him, the future is a source of inspiration that his students at Vives University of Applied Sciences, Hogeschool West-Vlaanderen and Luca School of Arts should indulge in to train their creativity and imagination. He lets his students digest tons of the better future literature, have fun with future-exploring games, but soon puts them into production mode. After all, in ten weeks' time, they have to build a future museum together in the metaverse. In doing so, Thomas activates a lot of skills that are systematically underused in education, but are indispensable for a future-proof career: creative collaboration, storytelling, design thinking and the use of digital tools.

IKEA | AN AI-POWERED JOURNEY INTO 2030

*What if, in the house of the future,
the best of ecology and technology are fused?*

In their 10th IKEA Life at Home Report, the future unfolds as a tableaux vivant. Thanks to a collaboration with Art Director Per Eriksson and the help of Generative AI, three future scenarios have been visualised around the lives of the fictional characters Jin, Angela and Jamie. The scenarios introduce intriguing stories, such as holographic home parties that bring together friends from far away, organic wallpaper with a layer of living algae to generate

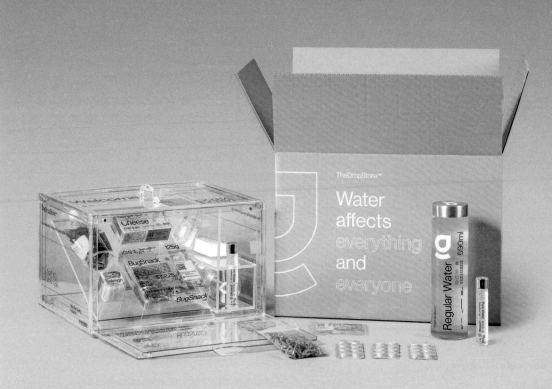

electricity from sunlight, and mycelium composite chairs that you can model on the screen and grow to your size in a controlled manner.

UN WATER CONFERENCE | THE DROPSTORE

What if the price of water was ten times higher tomorrow than it is today?

In our country, reliable and drinkable water comes straight from the tap, but for 3.6 billion people in the world, this is not the case. The Dropstore is a fictional supermarket that helps you imagine a world where drinking water has become so extremely expensive that most everyday products have become total luxury. One-gram cubes of cheese, pizza in the shape of a pill, bottled water with rusty brown content... The packaging of the products in the Dropstore always explains how regional water scarcity leads to economic shocks that can be felt and seen in your kitchen. The Dropstore was open to the public during the very first United Nations Water Conference in New York.

FLEMISH FIRE BRIGADE NETWORK | OPERATION FRONTDRAFT

What if new technologies led to unimaginably new emergencies?

The future offers all kinds of opportunities for aid organisations such as the fire brigade, but undoubtedly also brings with it many emergencies that are unthinkable, sometimes unimaginable, but in any case undesirable. Commissioned by the Flemish fire brigade network, together with the future-exploratory design studio Pantopicon, I developed a board game with which people from the entire hierarchy of the fire brigade can discover new technologies, tools, organisational forms, jobs, but also quite dystopian emergencies. You play against each other in teams and win a game round if you have performed the smartest operation to brave disasters that you could not have imagined in your wildest dreams.

What if, in the near future,
we remove the cow from our food chain?

After the takeover of the Vegetarian Butcher by Unilever, founders Jaap
Korteweg and Niko Koffeman focused on a crucial piece of Dutch heritage:
cheese. While waiting to decipher the code to use their robot cow Margaret –
a bioreactor – to convert freshly cut grass into casein (the protein for cheese),
they opened a nostalgic cheese shop in *'vegan capital'* Ghent with style. This
is where their plant-based cheeses – *Fromances* – such as Cream Passionel
and the herbal gem Garlic & Herb Affair were presented, which were then
available nationwide in supermarkets. The temporary pop-up shop mainly
served as a foretaste of a future in which, thanks to biotechnology, cheese can
be made without the intervention of cows. If the Netherlands were to focus
the same willpower on food technology as it does on renewable energy, the
Netherlands could immediately seize the position of world leader, according
to vegan cowboy Jaap Korteweg.

THE THIRD LUNG | THE FUTURE OF OUR FIRM

What if tomorrow everyone gets to choose
whether to work from home or come to the office?

Will people find their way back to the office in droves after the pandemic?
Or will working from home become the new normal? Will we continue to
embrace tools that digitally connect colleagues and teams to their work? Or
are we struggling with digital indigestion and craving physical and analogue
contact again? In the immediate aftermath of the pandemic, these were the
critical uncertainties that kept not only HR professionals and employers,
but also office fitters, architectural firms and property developers awake at
night. For De Derde Long, a coalition of construction companies involved in
office construction, we moderated an exploration of the future of work to find
nuance in the uncertainty at the time. The result consisted of a downloadable
white paper with guidelines that advocated resilience and agility: flexible
building and furnishing with modular and circular materials and designs to
promote mental and physical health in the office.

What if the Earth itself drew the map of the world?

We recognise the world map based on our Geography lessons. Nation-state borders are the result of thousands of years of war, marriage politics and diplomacy. But what if we were to divide the world with a non-human view? The annual migratory routes of geese or whales, the wanderlust of wolves, the range of the Northern Taiga or the habitat of the eel, ... It may be a matter of nature where our cultural-historical boundaries lie. Nature organisation 'One Earth' lived up to its name with a new atlas project. She divided the planet into 185 bioregions: contiguous ecoregions that, according to bioregionalists, offer a new view of the Earth and can make its management regenerative, more self-sufficient and more equitable.

NEW HEROES FOUNDATION | FICTIONAL EXPERTS

What if keynote speakers at conferences were replaced by actors?

As a welcome variation on public speakers, creative jack-of-all-trades Lucas de Man and his New Heroes Foundation created four fictional experts, played by actors, to send to conferences and congresses with a theatrical reading. Rodin Sharp, HR expert, gives us a glimpse into happiness in the workplace, Chris Everlast talks to his deceased wife about eternal life, Joop Meesters questions the future of value creation, money and 'our system' and Dr Makhlouf uses synthetic biology to tackle desertification. With his fictional experts, Lucas De Man investigates whether you can target scientific insights, established convictions, beckoning visions of the future, but also persistent worldviews much more penetratingly than when real entrepreneurs and experts do so.

THE URBAN VILLAGE PROJECT |
AN INTEGRAL OUTLOOK ON LIVING

*What if urban planners started working
with digital construction kits?*

The Urban Village Project, a speculative design exercise by Space 10, is a bold
vision of living in the face of climate change. The project embraces climate
neutrality, quality of life and affordability as core principles. On a digital
platform, blueprints for various urban functions (from apartments to retail
spaces and bicycle parking) are offered as digital twins. They are the digital
manuals for construction kits that consist of bio-based and modular building
materials. Funding from cities and pension funds makes housing flexible
and affordable, with options for residents to build up housing rights as a new
form of ownership. The Urban Village Project was presented disguised as a
fictional, but realistic real estate project with accompanying website, artistic
renders and models and was the brainchild of the now closed, but forever
legendary creative incubator Space 10.

'History doesn't repeat itself,
but it does rhyme.'

———

MARK TWAIN

NUTRITION: THE SINGULARITY SUPERMARKET

How can we make sustainable and healthy eating habits easy and attractive?

For a challenger in the European supermarket landscape, a small team of us went in search of innovation perspectives on sustainability and health for the next ten years.

Its market position as a price fighter did not make that easy. The consumers of this supermarket are particularly sensitive to prices and promotions, and the pricing of products that perform better in terms of sustainability was already quite sharp.

The trends that emerged on the horizon of the distribution sector at the time were well documented. The focus on healthy and sustainable products has been increasing for a long time. So has the need for transparency around nutritional value, provenance and sustainability performance. There was the fight against excess packaging and a growing variety of plant-based meat substitutes. During the pandemic, there was a huge acceleration in the growth of home deliveries. Challenging entrants to the market started delivering meal boxes to the living room without physical stores. A significant turn in consumer behaviour that should definitely not be a blind spot was the increasing need for control over the household budget. Price inflation was already being felt at the time. The cheap food prices of yesteryear would not come back.

Despite reasons to keep their feet on the ground, the team paid particular attention to the so-called Blue Zones, the five regions in the world where people age significantly more healthily thanks to good lifestyle habits and the report 'Nutrition in the Anthropocene' (The Lancet/EAT Foundation, 2019) that figured out how we can eat tasty and healthy food with 10 billion people without sacrificing the health of the planet.

THE NEW-KIDS-ON-THE-BLOCK

During future-exploratory workshops, we always make use of 'shining examples': usually start-ups that come 'from the bottom up' to disrupt the prevailing model of a sector with something completely new. The following initiatives received a lot of attention in the team:

- Loopstore, the Canadian circular ecosystem that connects consumers, supermarkets and A-brands in the delivery of groceries in premium, reusable packaging.
- Notpla, the British newcomer with edible and biodegradable food and drink packaging made from seaweed extracts.
- reNature, the Dutch agency commissioned by food multinationals such as Nestlé to help farmers all over the world make the transition to regenerative agriculture.
- The American company Habit Food Personalized, which puts together a diet and meal kits based on your DNA
- Kiwibot is a company that, thanks to AI, GPS technology and sensors, wants to deliver to the pavement with autonomous driving carts and thus reduce 65% of the delivery costs.
- The Australian Revo Foods, which uses 3D printing technology to imitate the flaky structure of salmon and already fills store shelves today, plant-based products full of umami.

TASTE ORGASM AND GOOSEBUMPS

But it was in the group that the most excitement arose around an observation outside the sector. Japan's Singularity Sushi in Tokyo claims to be the most high-tech restaurant in the world. You reserve a place by sending in your DNA sample, so that Singularity Sushi would 3D print personalised sushis with plant-based raw materials from the sea that would lead to a true taste orgasm.

The idea gave the group goosebumps and led to quasi-spontaneous analogy thinking: what makes this example so fascinating? And if a singularity sushi restaurant is possible, is there also a prospect for a singularity supermarket? Dozens – existing innovation examples were put together like pieces of a puzzle and that suggested that they were. Plant-based dairy substitutes such as Modest, Mylk and Joi already supply almond and oat milk in paste and powder form. The very first food printer, the Foodini conquered the counter-top of foodies to print pastas, pasta, chocolate and edible sculptures. Crisp was fully engaged in rolling out a much more local, seasonal and alternative food system across the Netherlands and Belgium with meal boxes, groceries and freshly prepared meals.

Of course, there were critical uncertainties. Was the home delivery market going to develop at the current pace? Or would we find our way back to the familiar supermarket en masse once the pandemic has been forgotten? And what about ecology and health? Will there be a nostalgic return to 'real food', driven by a pastoral longing for grandmother's time and distrust of what science and technology will conjure up on our plates? Or will we embark on the adventure of embracing so-called 'novel foods'? Will products of cellular agriculture (food made from raw materials produced in a bioreactor with microorganisms) appeal to us and will we welcome them in our diet?

MORE CONTROL OVER HEALTH, WALLET AND PLANET

Will we also drive around the pavement with unmanned cars at knee height, shopping and meals? Shall we curate dishes layer by layer based on customers' health profile? Are we going to accept meat from stem cells? And will we soon no longer be talking about our consumers, but about 'our subscribers'? No one has a crystal ball and the future cannot be predicted, but imagined.

The team concluded that new technologies show a credible perspective for the establishment of a true 'food service discounter' where more can be taken care of with fewer products, and where meal kits and freshly prepared dishes can be used to link a more climate-oriented diet to more health and offer more control over family spending.

NINE FUTURE-INSPIRED
FOOD CONCEPTS

CHLOÉ RUTZERVELD | CULINAIR CELLULAIR

*How can we familiarise the general public
with cellular agriculture?*

The speculative installation 'Culinair Cellular' by Eindhoven-based food designer Chloé Rutzerveld invites visitors to explore their culinary delights. This interactive installation intuitively guides you through a process in which emotions towards food and skepticism towards new food concepts are challenged. In the cell library, participants experiment with unusual combinations such as the cells of an old pear variety, an extinct animal (mammoth meatball, anyone?) and a protein-rich freshwater algae. They then choose a growth method to determine texture and structure, prepare the cell culture in the bioreactor and select a preparation method. The culinary adventure was launched at the Lowlands music festival to treat the widest possible audience to an eye-opening reflection on the future of our diet.

ANDERNACH | THE VERY FIRST EDIBLE CITY

What if the whole city was edible?

In Andernach, a German town on the Rhine, all urban greenery was gradually replaced by annuals, perennials, shrubs, shrubs and trees where there is something to snack on everywhere among the foliage. The beauty of food forests in the city is not only their feasibility, but also their unpredictability. There are no standard apples on trees that you also find in the supermarket. You will find forgotten fruit varieties, herbs with which you can garnish exclusive cocktails or hops with which residents brew their own city beer. There is no botanical racism here and exotic fruits such as the Citrus Trifoliata, the paw-paw tree, the prairie banana and the persimmon with its large fruits with jelly-like substance can simply be found, picked, sucked or spooned up here.

PIXELFARMING ROBOTICS |
PESTICIDE- AND HANDS-FREE ARABLE FARMING

What if robots cultivated a few square metres of arable land for each family?

In 2016, a group of engineers settled in an abandoned farm in the Dutch municipality of Olmskerk, North Brabant. Their mission: to develop regenerative precision agriculture as an alternative to the usual monoculture. After almost ten years of building prototypes, the Robot One was introduced: a robot on high wheels, equipped with cameras, sensors and tools for hands-free sowing, farming and harvesting. The robots virtually divide the arable land into square metres (pixels), sow a wide variety of vegetables, monitor soil quality, grow without pesticides and harvest without hands. Neighbouring families can reserve their pixel plots of land online to enjoy a weekly portion of fresh vegetables.

IVY FARM TECHNOLOGIES |
JAPANESE WAGYU SIRLOIN STEAK WITHOUT COW

What if we no longer needed farm animals to produce meat?

Quiz question: what consumes 70% of the world's freshwater resources, emits more CO_2 than all planes, cars and ships combined, caused 80% of deforestation this century and takes as many lives every thirty minutes as the entire Second World War combined? That's right, intensive livestock farming. And that justifies why we'd better see the next technological revolution on our plates. Oxford-based Ivy Farm Technologies has teamed up with the UK's largest meat producer Finnebrogue to produce the world's most expensive beef, the Wagyu steak, through cellular farming. Instead of growing a whole animal, specific cells are isolated and grown into edible products in a laboratory setting.

SAVOREAT | THE NESPRESSO MACHINE FOR HAMBURGERS

What if your next burger came out of a printer?

SavorEat, based in Rehovot, Israel, wants to turn the meat industry upside down with a 3D printer that will allow meatless burgers, and soon, steaks and seafood to be customised and prepared. Founder Barack Orenstein believes that decoupling livestock farming and fisheries, personalisation of food and on-demand production at the point of consumption can spark a revolution.

SavorEat has had successful restaurant pilots that have seen an increase in turnover and customer satisfaction. In addition to a network of robot chefs in restaurants, SavorEat sees a lot of potential in a home model, similar to a Nespresso machine.

LENTELAND FOUNDATION | RESTORING TIES WITH FARMERS

What if we could directly reconnect citizens and farmers?

The Dutch ASN Bank is an important linchpin in the wheel of the Lenteland Foundation, which on the one hand helps Dutch farmers to make the switch to regenerative agriculture and on the other hand wants to help them develop a new business model where consumers buy products directly from farmers in their neighbourhood as a cooperator or subscriber. Land is bought, farmers are sought and retrained as future farmers. The four very first community farms where experiments are being carried out are the Starckxhoeve in Belgium, Erve Kiekenbos and farm 't Gagel in the Dutch province of Gelderland and farm Sierveld in Mechelen in South Limburg. The goal is to optimise the formula in such a way that by 2030 there will be about 100 regenerative Spring Countries in Belgium and the Netherlands.

What if we ate healthily on prescription?

If U.S. family doctors were to prescribe fresh fruits and vegetables to vulnerable families and people with diabetes, $39.4 billion a year would be saved in the health economy and $4.8 billion in lost labour productivity. The U.S. population would also gain 260,000 healthy life years, according to Tufts University in Boston. Reason enough why doctors' offices associated with the Mass General Brigham prescribe fruit and vegetables. Through the Giant Food Fresh Connect Debit Card, their patients can then purchase up to $100 worth of prescribed fruits and vegetables each month.

UNCOMMON CREATIVE STUDIO | YELLOW STICKERS AS AN INFLATION COOKBOOK

What if we gave people control over their household budgets with new technology?

To encourage us to cook healthily despite rising food prices, the London-based creative agency is putting yellow stickers on discounted products on store shelves. Through a mobile app like Google Lens, consumers can scan the stickers and see what other discounted products they make a tasty dish with. Consumers can add discounted items themselves, after which AI combines them into new dishes. The motto *'find a meal in every deal'* encourages consumers to pin the crisis on a fork, with yellow stickers as a source of inspiration for affordable meals.

*What if culinary experience nature were a treat
for your employees?*

Singapore-based DBS Bank is committed to the concept of food forests on a
tiny-forest scale, in the middle of Asian cities. The first *DBS Food Forest* was
launched in 2020 in Singapore's financial heartland, the Changi Business
Hub. This is where the fifty most popular Southeast Asian herbs and vegetables grow to provide employees with a daily farm-to-table experience. Edible
Garden City, specialised in urban farming, manages the DBS foodscapes and
has been transforming an 8,000 m² former prison into an urban farm since
2021. With the 30 by 30 campaign, Singapore aims to produce at least 30% of
local food within the city limits by 2030.

'The future of food
is not just about what we eat,
but also about how it's produced,
distributed, and consumed.'

———

MARK POST,
PROFESSOR OF VASCULAR PHYSIOLOGY AT MAASTRICHT UNIVERSITY
AND CO-FOUNDER OF MOSA MEAT

COALITION
OF THE WILLING

3
COALITION
OF THE WILLING

———

No matter the size of your organisation, you can't change the world on your own. A good vision of the future attracts other organisations to cultivate an 'alliance of the willing' around it. Work together with people and organisations within and outside your sector who have an interest in achieving that same vision of the future. With a 'coalition of the willing' you create your own power of change to rewrite the rules of the game.

+ EARTH +, THE FLEMISH ALLIANCE FOR NATURE BASED SOLUTIONS

How do we create a future for the farmer and the construction industry through collaboration?

ABOUT UNICORNS, ZEBRAS AND PHOENIXES

In the motley animal kingdom of start-ups, unicorns are the fabulous tech companies that quickly reach a valuation of one billion dollars or more. Iconic examples such as Facebook, Uber and Airbnb were hailed to the point

that financial valuation seemed to be the only measure of success. As a result, every young man in his twenties began to present himself to investors as a comet that would soon hit its market. Soon after, zebra companies entered the scene to redefine 'success'. They choose scale thanks to networks of collaboration (usually with other zebra companies) and pursue a balance of financial success and social impact. Examples such as the home care company Buurtzorg and The Vegetarian Butcher brought innovation to their sector and inspired an entire generation of impact entrepreneurs. Gigacorns, on the other hand, are newcomers – especially in cleantech – with the strategic goal of removing 1 million tonnes of CO_2 per year from the atmosphere. The term 'phoenix' is increasingly used for companies that realise $1 billion in *nature-based solutions* annually.

> Nature-based solutions are a colourful range of solutions
> in which the power of nature is used not only
> to curb climate change, but also to bring biodiversity,
> well-being and help the regional economy to flourish.

Phoenix do this by connecting a network of different companies in different sectors with nature. In such a collaboration, each activity contributes as much as possible to the restoration, renewal, enrichment and balance of ecological systems and social structures. A phoenix in the making is + Earth + (pronounced Earth Plus) who wants to conquer the world from Flanders with the help of one of nature's fastest growing green crops: The Cannabis Sativa Cultivars, or 'industrial hemp'.

HEMP, THE HISTORICAL SUPERHERO OF THE PLANT KINGDOM

Without hemp, the Netherlands might never have had their Golden Age, according to Frederik Verstraete, spiritual father of + *Earth* +. For the treasures from distant continents navigated our ports with sails and ropes made of hemp.

You can make four times more paper per hectare of hemp than with wood. It can grow almost anywhere in the world, requires little water, and no pesticides. If all clothing made with cotton today were made from hemp, you could eliminate 16% of all pesticides in the world. For just about every type of material, a biodegradable alternative with hemp is conceivable. Hempcrete is an emerging, climate-friendly alternative to concrete, and just before a witch hunt for hemp was unleashed in the US in the late 1930s – because of the spectre that entire populations would smoke themselves stoned – Henry Ford made his car bodies with biocomposite from hemp instead of steel, and drove his personal car on Hemp-Ethanol. You have no idea what was made from hemp in days gone by, but Frederik Verstraete wants to use it to make building materials with his + Earth + in the future.

Industrial hemp can be harvested twice a year, and yields between 16 and 20 tons of biomass per hectare. But its true grandeur lies in the air, from which it can extract a mind-boggling 30 tonnes of CO_2 per hectare and, thanks to photosynthesis, converts it into raw material for renewable building materials. By way of comparison: a petrol family car emits 1 tonne of CO_2 per 10,000 kilometres. 1 hectare of hemp therefore captures the emissions of 100,000 car kilometres.

The power of hemp goes further: like a true medicine man, it has a phytoremedial effect. In layman's terms: you can use it to purify air, soil and water from historical sins such as pollution with heavy metals, oil spills, solvents, organic substances, mercury and even the eternal sinners – *forever chemicals* – such as PFAS, a group of 15,000 chemicals that cannot be broken down in nature.

PURIFYING THE ATMOSPHERE WITH HEMP, POLISHING OUR HOMELAND AND MAKING BUILDING MATERIALS

In the forgotten lands around the port of Antwerp, more than 400 hectares of unused land are waiting to be remediated with hemp. Add to this the 4 to 5,000 places in Flanders with medium-sized PFAS pollution and kill five birds with one stone: you save the historically highly polluted Flemish soil, relieve Flanders' largest employer (the construction sector) of the nitrogen crisis and climate pressure, you capture tons of CO_2 and you rewrite the Flemish agricultural chapter with a new story as a facilitator of a local, biobased, and circular economy. Profit often manifests itself on various fronts at Nature Based Solutions and you read that right: the future of construction consists of cooperation with the farmer.

If we open our window to the world, an estimated 1.9 billion hectares of land are orphaned and depleted by deforestation, overgrazing, intensive agriculture or pollution. As far as Provotyping is concerned, + Earth + grows hemp on a modest scale on small fields near Mechelen and Sint-Niklaas. For example, + Earth + already presents public opinion, politicians and potential allies with a wide range of possibilities. A wide range of applications are being tried, ranging from insulation material, façade modules, traffic light poles, beauty products, packaging material, etc. even hemp beer.

+ EARTH + AS A MARKETPLACE FOR NATURE-BASED SOLUTIONS

A broad coalition is emerging around + Earth +, which focuses primarily on Flanders but dreams of global expansion.

- C-biotech, a subsidiary of construction company Cordeel, aims to be the largest producer of biobased building materials in the Benelux.
- In collaboration with partners such as VITO (Flemish Institute for Technological Research), dredging companies DEME and McKinsey, an alliance is being forged to promote innovative remediation technologies.
- Together with Microsoft, a digital marketplace is being designed where landowners, agricultural organisations, companies with biodiversity and climate objectives and bio-based materials and nature-based solutions start-ups can meet, enter into transactions, monitor projects and obtain nature compensation tokens.

Somewhere in a United Nations audit office, it was calculated that stabilisation of the climate is achievable by phasing out fossil fuels and investing some 1,100 billion dollars in global nature-based solutions between 2024 and 2050.

This investment includes:
- $360 billion in regenerative agriculture and food forests;
- $340 billion in reforestation and nature restoration;
- $160 billion in marine ecosystem restoration;
- $130 billion in nature conservation and;
- 110 billion dollars in soil management and protection, such as the fight against desertification.

While $1,100 billion may seem like an astronomical amount, it's less than the annual defence budget of China and the United States combined. Currently, 83% of investments in nature-based solutions are borne by governments. To achieve the intended goal, efforts need to quadruple, with governments having to initiate new frameworks, financing mechanisms and incentives to stimulate new investment and revenue models around nature-based solutions.

The technological brother of nature-based solutions for removing CO_2 from the atmosphere on a large scale is called CCS (Carbon Capturing & Storage). It involves various processes in which an immense industrial vacuum cleaner captures CO_2 at the emission source or washes it out of the air, and then stores it deep underground, often in abandoned oil or gas fields, where it usually comes from. Despite the decreasing costs due to economies of scale and technological innovation, a lot of research, including that of McKinsey Sustainability, shows that CCS is very unlikely to meet the immense challenge in the coming decades at a reasonable price compared to nature-based solutions, let alone that there are cross-connections with the creation of other natural values.

That is why we are once again raising a glass to nature and unsurpassed human ingenuity in order to forge new links with it. We are looking forward to the many new phoenixes, nature applied technologies and ENVAIs (Environmental Artificial intelligence) that can help us *terraform* on our home planet.

'Every successful movement
in world history
is made up of a coalition.'

———

RUTGER BREGMAN

NINE HOPEFUL EXAMPLES
OF NATURE BASED SOLUTIONS

BEEODIVERSITY | 10,000 SURVEILLANCE DRONES
WITHOUT BATTERIES

How can we use nature to collect data?

According to the World Economic Forum, nature provides humans with
the equivalent of $125,000 billion in ecosystem services every year.
In that case, it is quite worthwhile to properly monitor that natural capital
in order to detect pollution of air, water and soil. Isn't it bizarre that until
recently there was no technology to surveil open space on a large scale? That's
why the Walloon Brabant-based BeeOdiveristy came up with the brilliant
idea of using bee colonies. The bees swarm, forage pollen and bring it to hives
equipped with hardware and software that can detect air and soil pollution
and changing biodiversity.

POSIDONIA OCEANICA | SWEAVING AWAY
650 MILLION TONNES OF CO_2 PER YEAR IN SEAGRASS

How can we increase the capacity of oceans to store carbon?

Posidonia oceanica is not an ordinary seaweed but a flowering plant that
forms fresh green carpets of grass on the seabed and absorbs carbon 35 times
faster than trees. During my holiday in Ibiza, I was enchanted by the gentle
spectacle of this swaying seagrass, which can be found from the Balearic
Islands in the Mediterranean Sea to Australia. Coastal ecosystems such as
seagrass, salt marshes, kelp forests, and mangrove forests are crucial for carbon storage because they can sequester carbon in the seabed for thousands
of years. Protection and restoration of Posidonia can sequester 650 million
tonnes of CO_2 annually, equivalent to total global shipping emissions. That is
why the World Bank is developing a framework so that companies can invest
in Blue Carbon credits to contribute to natural carbon storage.

BEEHOMES | HOMES OF FARMERS IN THE MIDDLE OF THE NETHERLANDS

How can we build houses with locally grown raw materials?

Only alternatives to concrete, steel and cement can reduce emissions from the construction sector. This convinced the brothers Luc and Wout de Wit to sow their fields with elephant grass, sunflower, sorghum and fibre hemp. A mobile factory makes a semi-finished product on site from the harvest, with which you can make a wide variety of building materials. With the first harvest, blow-in insulation will be made for Dutch houses. The second harvest goes to the first Beehomes, which are 90% biobased and on balance 50 tonnes of CO_2 negative. The construction farmers want to show that you can breathe a regenerative life into the construction sector locally, from seed to home.

ANT FOREST | REGENERATIVE REAL LIFE GAMING

How can we use the smartphone to reward sustainable behaviour?

Ant Forest, the regenerative project of Ant Group (the mobile payment arm of Chinese e-commerce giant Alibaba), takes users into a real-life game to inspire them to go green. Eco-conscious purchases and sustainable commuting result in points that allow Ant Forest to plant real trees in Chinese reforestation projects. Since 2016, it has already attracted more than 550 million users and planted more than 220 million trees. Ant Forest demonstrates the power of mobile technology in influencing behaviour and engaging people in regenerative initiatives. For several years now, China has been working with a 'gross ecological product' that measures the value of nature.

OYSTER HEAVEN | THE SEABED AS
A PURIFICATION PLANT

How can we use nature to restore marine ecosystems?

80% of all sewage in the world ends up in the sea untreated, increasing acidification, nitrogen levels and algae explosions in the water. Oysters are powerful water filters that filter about 200 litres per day. Oyster beds are natural purification plants, nursery grounds for marine life, and the basis for a healthy ecosystem. To allow nature and fish stocks in coastal areas to flourish again, Rotterdam's Oyster Heaven is once again constructing oyster beds with biodegradable blocks that are provided with oyster seed. They do this together with local fishermen and companies that want to offset their carbon footprint.

HANDPRINT.TECH | FROM NEGATIVE FOOTPRINT
TO POSITIVE HANDSHAKE

How do we connect companies with nature restoration?

In faraway Singapore, expatriate academic, sustainability consultant and Fleming Simon Schillebeeckx is developing the digital platform handprint. tech to help companies establish a regenerative relationship with nature. His vision is that reducing the negative impact of companies is not enough. In addition, the resilience of the afterhours must also be considerably restored and expanded. To help with that, companies can browse a digital catalogue of nature restoration projects from Brazil to Indonesia by handprint. With the *'Regenerative Target Calculator'*, companies can digitally compose their positive handshake with nature, live up to it and create their new narrative around impact.

RRREEFS | BUILDING CORAL REEFS WITH LEGO BLOCKS

What if we restore coral reefs with building blocks?

Coral reefs, the architects of the sea, not only form a shield that dampens 97% of wave power to protect coastlines, but are also the birthplace of 25% of all marine life. The Swiss company Rrreefs focuses on design, science and education to involve us in the restoration of coral reefs. With their beautiful, 3D-printed building blocks in terracotta, they can not only build structures with precision. They also control important properties such as surface structure and alkaline content. Thanks to the playful nature of their building blocks, they can involve tourists, local organisations and companies in their projects in an accessible way.

NATURE BASED SOLUTIONS INSTITUTE | THE 3-30-300 RULE FOR HIGH-QUALITY URBAN GREEN SPACES

There are no less than five reasons to welcome more greenery and water in cities. More nature in the city forms a shield to protect city dwellers from an increasingly erratic climate. It ensures more biodiversity, thriving, valuable neighbourhoods, more spontaneous contact between people, less crime and an invigorating effect on our mental health. To speed up the latter, Cécil Koni-jnendijk, founder of the Nature Based Solutions Institute, came up with the 3-30-300 rule: Each of us must look out at least 3 trees, 30% of a residential area must find shelter under foliage and everyone must find a lush green area for relaxation at 300 metres. More and more cities are embracing the 3-30-300 rule as a signpost towards future-proofing.

JEFFREY MARLOW | RESTORING THE EARTH WITH EXTREMOPHILES

Bacteria and fungi offer an interesting register of medicines to provide environmental problems with the right treatment. In 2018, a group of scientists led by biologist Jeffrey Marlow embarked on a daring expedition to Ambrym Island in the Atlantic Ocean. Their goal: to investigate microbial life that can thrive in the hottest places on Earth. The Marum crater, with its 7.4-kilometre-wide lake of boiling lava, served as a research site for extremophiles: microorganisms that can survive in extreme conditions. The results not only have implications for understanding *terraforming* (creating life on other planets), but also offer applications for terrestrial challenges such as restoring farmlands and purifying highly polluted water supplies.

'If you have the ability
to turn another planet into Earth,
then you also have the ability
to turn Earth back into Earth.'

———

NEIL DEGRASSE TYSON,
AMERICAN ASTROPHYSICIST AND STORYTELLER

PROVOTYPING STEP 2
—
CREATE A COALITION OF THE WILLING

Your organisation is not likely to change the world on its own. The good news is that this visionary view of yours has the potential to attract like-minded organisations. Around that vision, you can form an 'alliance of the willing' and together create a context where cooperation is nurtured, innovation is stimulated and where the rules of the game can be rewritten. Here are four more questions to answer with your team via the Provotyping canvas.

THE AMMUNITION ROOM

What are the key skills, resources,
and strengths we need to realise our vision?

Dive into reality with your team to create that singularity supermarket, that alliance of building farmers or realise your own dream scenario. What resources, skills and other assets are needed for this? What should be in your ammunition room?

Participants can work individually, fill a series of sticky notes and as a team you can use the decision tree to a list of essential, strategic building blocks.

ALLIES

Who are the 'usual suspects',
but especially the 'unusual suspects' for our alliance?

Organisations naturally tend to work with the same organisations over and over again. The bonds are forged, you can look back on a history, and the trust is there. The risk of sitting down with the same players over and over again is that you don't open windows to let in new oxygen. Regime players in particular also tend to perpetuate themselves rather than question themselves. Yet you often see successful coalitions when existing regime players do not want to miss the train of the future, step into the pool and put their sound power, scope and expertise to the test. New-kids-on-the-block, but also independent experts, artists and designers can breathe a breath of fresh air and feed the coalition with new lines of thought and perspectives. An important condition should be that allies in your '*coalition of the willing*' follow the principles of open innovation and start working together in a mode of generosity.

Make a list with your team of usual suspects, but especially unusual suspects and always motivate why you would involve a certain party.

CASE BELLI

What are the motivations of our would-be allies to join?

For organisations, there are a lot of reasons why it's much more comfortable to keep doing what they're doing. There are also a lot of reasons why it's hard to switch to something new: am I even capable of doing so? Do I have faith in that new story and the people who carry it in their banner? Can I afford that change? What will others think of me? What is the risk of punishment?

What are the motivations and barriers, dreams and fears of our allies to join?

Take a look at the figure above and try to answer the following four questions:
- Pain: What pressures, frustrations, discomfort and shortcomings does the organisation experience today in the existing world?
- Gain: What does the organisation have to gain from maintaining that new world? What makes it comfortable today?
- Dreams: What are the benefits of embracing this new worldview?
- Fears: What insecurities, prejudices and fears prevent the organisation from embracing this new worldview?

These frameworks will help you and your team map out the motivations of your allies. Not only will they feel better seen, heard and understood, you will also be able to put them in a role where they can flourish to the best of themselves.

THE STRONGHOLD

Which location would be the best strategic position
for our 'coalition of the willing'?

As a coalition, it is better to have a regular appointment and physical location for meetings. Despite most members of the Blue Cluster being located in the city of Antwerp, it has its headquarters in Ostend, close to its field of activity: the open sea. The Port of Rotterdam's coalition of the willing on climate-neutral shipping has its annual international meeting on the sidelines of the Recharge Earth conference in Amsterdam. Strategically choosing a time and place (physical or digital) gives your coalition a common ground and home. Which one would be a strong choice for your team?

OUR PIONEERING ALLIANCE

What would you call our 'coalition of the willing'?

Finally, choose a good name for the alliance. Baptising your initiative with a name gives it an identity in one move and makes it easy for the participants to create a connection with it.

TJOKVOL
CIRCULAIR
BOUWMATERIAAL

KOZIJNEN	8 %
GLAS	2 %
HANG- EN SLUITWERK	1 %
BRANDBLUSMIDDELEN	1 %
BETON	45 %
KERAMIEK	6 %
DAKBEDEKKING	3 %
KABELGOTEN	1 %
KABELS- EN LEIDINGEN	2 %
SCHAKELMATERIAAL	1 %
NOODSTROOMVOORZIENING	1 %
LUCHTBEHANDELING	1 %
GIPSTOEPASSINGEN	5 %
DEUREN	4 %
VLOERAFWERKINGEN	7 %
GEVELBEPLATING	5 %
VERLICHTINGSARMATUREN	2 %
CV KETELS	2 %
KEUKENS	3 %

NEW HORIZON ZIET DE STAD ALS BRON.
DE GEBOUWDE OMGEVING IS ONS MAGAZIJN.
EN ZIJ VOL BRUIKBARE GRONDSTOFFEN. WIJ
ONTMANTELEN GEBOUWEN MET BEHOUD
GRONDSTOFFEN.

NINE STRATEGIC EXAMPLES OF COALITION BUILDING

AUPING | GENEROUS SLEEP REVOLUTIONS

Assembly, disassembly, take-back logistics, material composition, etc. With a large alliance of no less than 40 organisations, royal bed maker Auping has undergone a remarkable acceleration in 2022 from one circular mattress to a completely new range of beds, bed bases and mattresses. In addition, Auping put some of its most successful products on hold forever. The journey to a circular future is not without sacrifices, and principles are only really principles if they bring inconvenience, sustainability director Mark Groot Wassink aptly notes. Auping shows that if you transform your linear value chain into a collaborative ecosystem, you can significantly accelerate the process towards a circular economy.

ARCADIS | CHANGE STARTS FROM WITHIN

Cities cover only 3 to 5% of the earth's surface, but they contribute to 50% of waste and up to 60% of greenhouse gases. The production of cement and concrete is responsible for 10 to 12% of carbon emissions. The design of cities therefore has a major impact on a planet – for a positive future. That is why a vanguard of 'Pioneers of Change' at the Belgian branch of the engineering firm Arcadis worked for a year on a programme to give every 'Arcadian' every power as a sustainability ambassador in construction projects. The offer – 'skill up, speak up, act up' – shows how a small alliance can transform a large organisation from within, according to director and initiator Rik Menten.

NEW HORIZON | HARVESTING AND INVENTING BUILDING MATERIALS

Putting your mission first is a fundamental precondition for 'coalition of the willing'. And for New Horizon, it sounded like 'making the construction industry waste-free'. Well anchored in a network of established names in the construction world, New Horizon became the director in the Netherlands of both material cycles (The Urban Mining Collective) and design assignments (The Circular Design Collective), resulting in many pioneering market breakthroughs. What is special is that New Horizon uses its own language. They don't talk about demolition, but about harvesting materials and every building is seen as a material donor. Today, the coalition has evolved into what they call a 'Native Circular Company'. At its base is still an ecosystem of organisations that all embrace the same circular philosophy.

NATURALIS | GREEN MEETING TABLES FOR SCIENCE AND BUSINESS

The general public knows Naturalis mainly for its beautiful museum in Leiden, which receives 400,000 visitors a year, and its imposing skeleton of the T-Rex. Few people know that Naturalis houses the 4th largest collection of natural history artefacts in the world and has been conducting scientific research into nature for 200 years. This research is no longer carried out in an ivory tower, but through 'Green Circles' in collaboration with companies such as Heineken, KPMG and Alliander. These collaborations bring science and business together in a generous exchange: Naturalis shares knowledge about how companies can build positive relationships with nature, while companies ensure that Naturalis fulfils its mission: to put scientific knowledge about nature into action all over the world.

FASCINATING | THE EUROPEAN AGRICULTURAL REVOLUTION STARTS IN GRONINGEN

Fascinating from Groningen distinguishes itself as a pro-movement to shape agricultural transition, rather than a conservative farmers' syndicate to protect the sector from innovation. The platform, led by director Tjeerd Jongsma, encourages farmers to find their way to a regenerative agricultural system. Because of this extensive ambition, we work together with major players such as Friesland Campina, Agrifirm Avebe, Cosun and a long series of government agencies and knowledge institutions. The dot on the horizon: more health per hectare. As a first achievement, their 'agri-food-nature Transition Model' was calculated financially and ecologically and translated into a series of innovative pilot projects. The challenge for Fascinating lies in removing uncertainties, so that thousands of farmers in the Netherlands and worldwide find the courage to innovate.

When it comes to greenery in the city, many organisations in the Netherlands are historically rooted in forest and park management. Because green infrastructure is vital in future-proofing public space, and is therefore much more than beautification, Joost Verhaegen – aka the Dutch Boominee – founded a podcast to connect prominent academics, urbanists, psychologists and sociologists around the question of how to pave the way towards nature-inclusive cities. As is often the case, a podcast is a good antenna to broaden, deepen and connect knowledge and relationships around a theme. As a side-kick in the podcast, I experience how numerous ideas and initiatives have already emerged from the recordings.

SEOUL | THE MORE WE SHARE, THE MORE WE HAVE

As early as 2010, Seoul formulated the vision of becoming the world capital of the sharing economy. Cars, bicycles, equipment, office space, ... The government provides a data platform where more than five thousand data types about the activities of 10 million inhabitants are collected. In this way, entrepreneurs can develop sharing services to their heart's content. Apart from the data infrastructure, the foundation consists mainly of 'Pumasi', the deeply embedded view in South Korean culture that states that 'the more we share, the more we have'. It is a striking example with which I was able to inspire souls at VLAO's Living Lab Rent and Sharing, where a coalition of entrepreneurs wants to increase not only purchasing power, but also the sharing power in the economy.

MASCO | THE WEST FLEMISH COALITION ON MATERIALS-AS-A-SERVICE

According to Statbel, construction waste represents at least 30% of our Belgian waste mountain. With the support of VLAIO (Agency for Innovation and Entrepreneurship) and impact investor Piet Colruyt, no fewer than 20 producers of building materials from West Flanders are joining forces to set up what they call a 'MASCO'. Masco stands for a *'materials-as-a-service-company'* and would be responsible for the pre-financing, take-back and reintroduction of circular building materials. Logistics may be the final piece of the circular economy, but with the design of building materials you determine no less than 80% of your environmental impact. That is why MASCO, as a coalition, also chooses to bundle creative brainpower.

NEW INDUSTRY: THE BLUE CLUSTER

From 'Coalition of the willing' to 'Community of Practice'

Imagine that you, as a famous chef, want to use your fame to pay tribute to the rich, but unsurpassed treasure trove of salty delicacies from our coastal area. There are the oysters that you can forage yourself at low tide in Oosterschelde National Park. There are the mussels from bottom or hanging culture. But also the dozens of edible sea vegetables such as sea kale, beach beet, spoon leaf, samphire, oyster leaf, sea lavender, salty potatoes, odourless chamomile and the 28 edible seaweed species that flourish in the Eastern Scheldt and the North Sea.

AN UNDERWATER PICKING GARDEN

A creative brainstorm – while enjoying a sunny sea white beer brewed with kelp and crispy prawn crackers from knotted seaweed – leads to an outrageous idea: What if we developed an underwater picking garden? Here, families with children can discover the culinary delights of the sea during balmy summer days while snorkelling with a floating basket in shallow water. With their harvest, the chef could make tasty snacks ashore. It could become a new coastal attraction that connects tourism with ecology and gastronomy. Ideal city marketing.

But instead of trying to figure everything out on your own, it's better to join a coalition of the willing, such as the Blue Cluster. The Blue Cluster is an alliance of up to 180 member organisations that facilitates partnerships and co-innovation between Flemish companies to make a blue economy a reality. From engineering firms to university research groups, energy companies, robotics companies, financial institutions and biotech startups, ... The plumage of their members is very diverse, but one vision connects them all: for a climate-positive large-scale industry, we have to take to the sea. Because for the fossil raw materials, fuels, fertilisers, plastics and carbon-intensive farming techniques that we know from land, there is always a blue, renewable and alternative future scenario waiting at sea.

THE DUNNING-KRUGER ROLLERCOASTER

As is so often the case with new, never-before-seen ideas, almost everyone has to go through the *Dunning-Kruger process* with them. The process starts on top of your *'bullshit mountain'*: the idea feels great, you get a sense of adventure, you see it all in front of you and you consider yourself lucky with your originality. But then 'the valley of despair' soon follows: that will cost money! How do you make that profitable? Who is waiting for that and who has the space for it? Do we have to find an abandoned marina for that? A bungalow park on the Oosterschelde? Is that not possible in the Ostend Spuikom? Who has the extensive technical and scientific knowledge required for this? How do you build something like that? And what about permits? If you don't drop your idea in the valley of despair, you have to climb 'the slope of enlightenment' with it, and it takes a lot of work and effort.

The Blue Cluster is active in creating space and accelerating breakthroughs needed to develop a renewable economy at sea.

For climate-positive large-scale industry,
we need to take to the sea.

SIX BLUE INNOVATION PATHS

Today, the Blue Cluster is running more than sixty projects, divided into six innovation pathways: Blue Tourism, Renewable Energy, Coastal Protection, Maritime Connections, Ocean Pollution and Marine Nutrition. In each of these extensively documented innovation pathways (Blue roadmaps), a lot of research, expertise and infrastructure is available. The advantage of knocking on the door of the Blue Cluster is that you have all parties in the value chain to realise your blue economy project under one roof. That saves time and money.

For CEO Piet Opstaele, there are conditions attached to membership. You have to be progressive, show commitment that you want to make a positive impact and be willing to work according to the principles of *open innovation*.

SEVEN PRINCIPLES OF OPEN INNOVATION

1. By opening doors and windows to insights from research institutes, suppliers and other so-called 'external parties', you allow inspiration and creative energy to flow through your organisation.
2. By combining creativity, resources and experience with external parties, you break through organisational boundaries and arrive at much more robust solutions.
3. Effective open innovation requires a subtle, balanced but also generous attitude in the management of intellectual property.
4. Nurturing new connections between start-ups, academic institutions, and industry leaders creates fertile ground and an innovation ecosystem where ideas, technology, and market insights are readily exchanged.
5. Open innovation thrives best in an environment with flexible structures. Dedicated innovation labs, accelerators, co-creation sessions, and frequent moments of inspiration are important to nurture a culture of creative collaboration.
6. Open Innovation breaks down geographical constraints and provides organisations with unprecedented access to global markets.
7. A cultural transformation focused on appreciation with room for failure is essential to the success of open innovation. You create that kind of safe environment by valuing external contributions, embracing experimentation, and celebrating both successes and failures as learning moments.

During the first years of work, the six blue innovation paths were mainly explored in research mode by initiating projects around them and giving them all the space they need. Nowadays, everyone knows what an autonomous ship, or what a sea farm is. Today, the main focus is on levers, cross-connections and bundling effects in search of the right revenue models, acceleration and valorisation, according to Piet. We are a global player in offshore energy, but we are also developing leadership in nature-based solutions in Flanders. Piet likes to refer to cooperation with nature in the context of coastal protection such as 'Coast Busters'. These are projects that contain only positive elements and which now require economic modelling. Promoting this expertise internationally is an opportunity that we should not miss. After imagining that Blue future, we must now become frontrunners in realisation. The 'coalition of the willing' must now become a 'community of practice'.

MARIPARKS

In order to realise this 'community of practice', much more concrete frame-work and space must be created that stimulates innovation and blue entrepreneurship. Many investors are convinced of a blue economy, but the risks (not least administrative risks such as long permit processes) are high. Conditions at sea can be harsh. Therefore, the infrastructure must be robust and that costs money. Each initiative on open water easily costs 300,000 euros, and for an average start-up those costs are high. That is why the Blue Cluster is working on mariparks: nature-inclusive, low-regulation zones at sea where scientists and entrepreneurs are welcome to experiment and start. At sea, we don't have to think two-dimensionally, but we can think three-dimensionally. And as we learned in school: 10^2 is a hundred, but 10^3 is a thousand. That is why multi-use must become a starting point for economic activities at sea. By combining different activities (wind energy, green hydrogen production, seaweed cultivation, seafood production, etc.), you can create a space-efficient, logistical and cost-efficient ecosystem. Moreover, the development of marine parks fits perfectly with European and national strategies to promote a sustainable, blue economy and contribute to the blue pillar of the European Green Deal. Piet Opstaele is rather cautious with the metaphor of 'business park at sea'. What we have done spatially and ecologically wrong on land, we must not repeat at sea. In the blue economy, we need to look beyond the concept of sustainable and leapfrog into a regenerative mode.

SEA FARMS

With fish stocks under severe pressure worldwide, wild fishing has reached its limits, and the traditional, somewhat vague and hard-to-prove mindset of 'sustainable fishing' is also setting its limits. The perspective of sea farms shows the potential to produce much more food while establishing a regenerative, positive relationship with marine ecosystems and biodiversity. Today, more than 70% of our world's precious freshwater resources go to agriculture, horticulture and livestock farming. According to the World Bank, more than 40% of our earth's surface is currently devoted to agriculture. And the WHO (World Health Organization of the United Nations) has been saying for some time that with a rising world population, we will have to produce at least 50 to 70% more food in the next fifty years. Marine farming does not require fresh water, and food can be produced without pesticides and artificial fertilisers. In particular, large-scale cultivation of fast-growing, energy-rich and versatile macro-algae such as kelp removes CO_2 from the atmosphere and has a stabilising effect on the pH value (acidity) of the sea. Combination with other forms of aquaculture offers a worthy addition to food production on land, especially in the light of a growing world population.

For the general public, however, seaweed still has a pretty blubbery and slimy image. The emerging blue economy is largely far from sight and the activity is often literally located below the surface of the water. It therefore seems a long way off that the fruits of the blue economy will conquer our plates, our bathrooms and our wardrobes. An underwater picking garden would therefore be a nice provo type to let the general public experience the benefits of a blue economy. It is at the crossroads of three innovation paths: marine food, blue tourism and – who knows – also coastal protection. The underwater picking garden could provide a unique and educational experience where new, culinary discoveries can be celebrated in a Burgundian way.

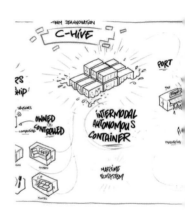

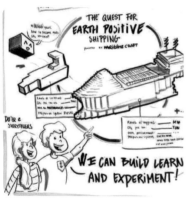

NINE EXAMPLES OF LIMITLESS POTENTIAL FOR THE BLUE ECONOMY

THE SEAWEED FARMERS | FISHING PORT BECOMES UNDERWATER VEGETABLE GARDEN

Nikki Spil and Sjoerd Laarhoven, aka The Seaweed Farmers, developed an underwater vegetable garden in the harbour docks of IJmuiden ten kilometres from my favourite holiday dunes. With steel mill Tata Steel's plumes of smoke in the background, they promote the versatility of macro algae. A seaweed farm acts as a greedy biofilter that removes phosphates, nitrates and nitrogen from the water, and serves as a breeding ground for fish. The harvest of 16,000 kg of seaweed is locally converted into bioplastics and 3D printer filament, and the rest is used as animal feed to reduce methane emissions from cows. As seaweed promoters and CO_2 binders, the seaweed farmers try to promote collaborations with companies. Their small underwater vegetable garden binds about 2.4 tonnes of CO_2 annually, equivalent to 27,000 car kilometres driven. As a promotion, their kelp weed is also used to brew the Sunny Sea White beer.

PORT OF ROTTERDAM | COALITION OF THE WILLING

Coalition of the willing. You probably first heard the term in George W. Bush's war rhetoric. In the context of sustainability transition, I heard it for the first time at the Port of Rotterdam. If those 35,000 ships a year were to enter and leave the port without emissions, it would easily save 13.7 million tonnes of CO_2. Nico Van Dooren, Director of New Business Development, formulated a dream for the future and formed a coalition around it with new market challengers, but also regime players such as Maersk, Shell, BP, CMA DGM and the Port of Singapore. You have to harness the expertise of that huge number of organisations and connect them to form a collaborative ecosystem. The annual Recharge Earth conference is an ideal place to give an annual state of affairs. As a coalition, we are working collectively on energy saving, energy transition to new energy sources and carriers, and the transition to a circular port in symbiosis with green chemistry.

STEERER | TACKLING FIVE TRANSITION CHALLENGES AT ONCE

Commissioned by Steerer, the European platform for Waterborne industries, my colleague Jan Leyssens and I were allowed to repeat the exercise for the context of the port of Antwerp. We invited about 100 tenors from the international shipping industry (shipping companies, but also energy start-ups and academics, etc.) and moderated a provotyping session around five transition challenges: energy transition, circular port and shipping, regenerative relationship with maritime biodiversity, but also automation and the battle for young talent. The proceeds consisted of radical, innovative ideas on traceability of impact and offsetting, industrial symbiosis with nature conservation, new modes of transport, modular ships, replaceable propulsion technology and energy storage, ... But the most important result was the insight that these five transition challenges are not isolated. The most relevant innovations are multipurpose. They address all five of the transition tasks at the same time.

SARGABLOCK | BRICKS FROM ALGAE EXPLOSIONS

Due to the run-off of fertilisers via rivers, you get ever larger algae explosions at sea. Instead of letting the mountains of Sargassum (a brown algae abundant in the Gulf of Mexico) rot along North American coasts, causing a lot of respiratory disorders, Omar Vasquez made a deal with hotel chains to clean up their beaches. The Sargassum is cleaned up, then mixed with clay and recycled bricks from demolition sites and processed into new bricks for house building.

COASTBUSTERS | COASTAL MANAGEMENT WITH NATURE

Traditional seawall engineering is reeling under the weight of maintenance, flood risks, and ecological damage as our coasts, ravaged by climate change, demand more and more protection. To find answers, we are increasingly looking to nature-inspired designs (NID). The aim of the Coastbusters is to involve nature as an ally in coastal protection while strengthening ecosystems and biodiversity. Crustaceans, cavity animals and plants that flourish in coastal areas play the leading role. They build biogenic reefs that not only prevent erosion but also contribute to coastal defence. With the blessing of the Blue Cluster, the Coastbusters are investigating this approach in Ostend and De

Panne in Belgium and want to share the findings worldwide for a much more nature-inclusive coastal management.

GREENWAVE | INTERNATIONAL NETWORK OF PERMACULTURE AT SEA

A few nautical miles from New York City and the Hudson Estuary, Bren Smith manages a sea farm consisting of vertical structures that grow mussels, oysters, kelp and scallops. The sea farm also functions as an artificial reef and nursery for up to 150 animal species. Bren Smith was once a fisherman and today considers himself a climate farmer. Not only does he want to bind a lot of CO_2 and engage in subsea permaculture. With his organisation Green Wave, he also wants to inspire fishing communities around the world to get started with *restorative ocean farming*. To promote marine farming to the general public, he processes kelp seaweed into kelp popsicles, kelplinguine and even kelp cocktails.

UNITED | DEMONSTRATING THE SCOPE OF MULTIPLE VALORISATION

Infrastructure at sea is expensive, so it makes a lot of sense to investigate how you can make the most of it with a wide variety of applications. Under the direction of the Blue Cluster , the Horizon 2020 project UNITED embraces this challenge, with a focus on the multiple exploitation of the sea through solid demonstration projects. In Belgium, within the Belwind offshore wind farm, a pilot is underway for the cultivation of flat oysters and sugar algae. Special hanging culture systems are being tested in the rough sea in the Westdiep zone. Wind turbine erosion protection with guided reef growth of young oysters is also being examined. This Belgian model, where energy production, food production and recovery come together, beautifully illustrates the multiple use of space, infrastructure and labour at sea.

POSHYDON | GREEN HYDROGEN PLANT AT SEA

A broad collaboration between NEL Hydrogen, TNO, InVesta, Hatenboer, Gasunie, DEME, Eneco and a long list of other organisations resulted in a world first in the North Sea with the very first national green hydrogen plant.

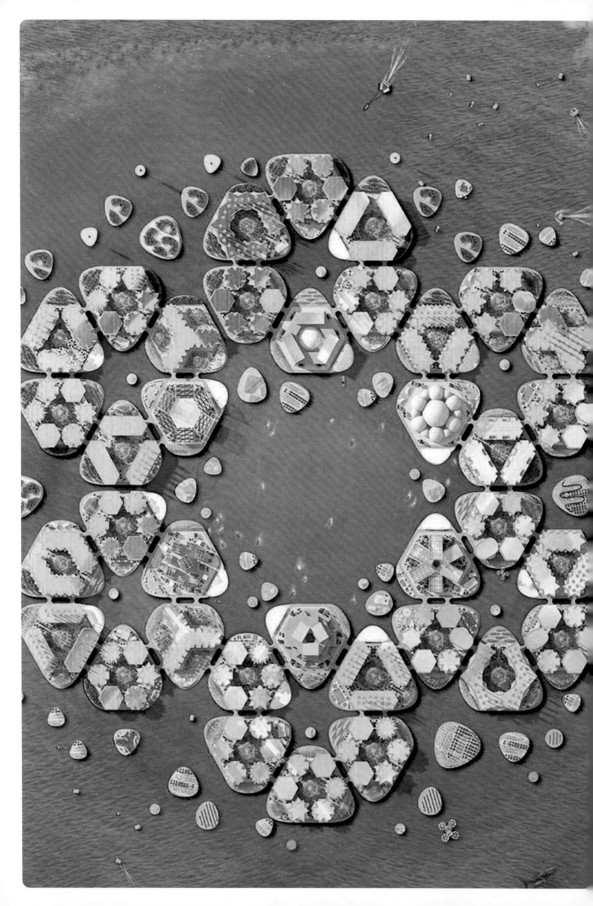

More and more wind farms are being built at sea, and also further and further from the coast. Through electrolysis of seawater, you can convert electricity into hydrogen during production peaks, store it and transport it via existing gas pipelines. The hydrogen plant is set up on the Q13a oil and gas platform about ten nautical miles off the coast of Scheveningen. It is a bit symbolic: a relic of the old economy stands as a flagpole for the new one. The fact that there are many platforms in the North Sea that are at the end of their lifespan offers a particularly interesting perspective.

PWN | CLIMATE BUFFERS IN VIRTUAL REALITY

In the past century, we mainly used energy-guzzling brute force in drinking water production to disconnect ourselves from nature. PWN, the North Holland drinking water company, is now investigating how it can meet the growing demand for drinking water together with nature. One ambition is the construction of a climate buffer – a created nature reserve – in the IJsselmeer, the inland sea behind the Afsluitdijk, which is also known as the Dutch bathtub. The aim is to collect, store and purify fresh water in harmony with biodiversity, coastal protection and space for tourism. A 3D model ensures that various what-if scenarios can be applied to the plan, but also enables virtual reality animations to allow policymakers, recreationists and local residents to experience this new, constructed nature reserve.

OCEANIX | FLOATING SDG CITIES

According to the World Economic Forum's Global Risks Report, as many as 570 coastal cities and 800 million people are exposed to rising sea levels at a global temperature rise of 2°C. The Danish architectural firm BIG (Bjarke Ingels Group), MIT Center for Ocean Engineering, UN-Habitat, Busan Metropolitan City, Arup, and Korea Maritime & Ocean Univeristy are therefore working together on a floating and modular city. The seventeen Sustainable Development Goals of the United Nations are used as draft guidelines. In contrast to a traditional master plan that divides an area with buildings and paving, the urban metabolism of water, material, energy flows and food production was the planning starting point here. Oceanix now considers itself a bluetech company, and the first prototype of Oceanix for 10,000 residents will open off the coast of the Korean city of Busan in 2025.

PROVOTYPING

4
PROVOTYPING

—

It is very important that your coalition of the willing frees your vision of the future from the meeting room as soon as possible. So that people can really experience it, we translate it into a visible and tangible 'provocative prototype': we gently do violence to the existing, and hold up the mirror to something new. Add some wonder to the experience and magic happens: you open minds to renewal and turn on the creative light.

People are going to get it as soon as they see it. Build it, and they will follow.

THE MICROBIAL SNACK VENDING MACHINE

In the future, nature will be our operating system and micro-organisms such as algae and bacteria will be the new apps.

When you enter the immense, concrete, saucer-shaped UFO of 77 metres in diameter, you immediately bump into the slanted parked silver-gray DMC DeLorean sports car in which Marty McFly and Dr Emmett Brown travel through time in the film *Back to the Future* (1985). If you then stand in the middle of the belly of the spaceship and look up, you will see four ring-shaped floors: the Geosphere, the Biosphere, the Technosphere and the Mindsphere. We have to be on the fourth floor. Here, among many other installations, we find '*The microbial vending machine*', loosely translated: the microbial snack machine.

To make the elusive microbial life around us visible, but also to make the future prospects of biotechnology clear to the general public, organic designer Emma Van der Leest designed the microbial snack machine. When you stand in front of the solid installation, you can quickly suspect what is going on. It seems as if a discarded, Dutch FEBO croquette-from-the-wall machine has been saved from demolition and upgraded to a device to distribute other products. There are four columns, each with eight removal gates, respectively for algae, bacteria, fungi and enzymes (proteins that accelerate biochemical changes). Behind each gate is a transparent, flat petri dish containing a dingy biochemical culture under a lamp.

On the right-hand side of the device is a legend in large letters of what you can do with it: produce bio-based bricks, 'grow' vegan quality leather, ferment biokerosene, brew natural dyes for textiles, knit new generations of plastic polymers, grow a juicy hamburger, ... All neatly with the Latin name of the micro-organism in question that can serve as a biochemical factory.

Is this an archaeological artifact from a not-so-distant future where you can hatch all kinds of materials yourself at home? With a home-garden-and-kitchen bioreactor? What it certainly does is translate a possible future into an experience. What is unimaginable to many becomes tangible here.

We are here in the fascinating territory of *'speculative design'*, a progressive design approach that ventures into the unseen, the as yet non-existent, but expected to be the reality that is not plucked out of thin air. The future is not predictable, but it is imaginable. And that is why every installation and intervention in this building serves as a catalyst for our imagination. With its futuristic and iconic shape of a spaceship, the Evoluon is an important landmark in the city of Eindhoven. Evoluon was built as a Philips technology museum in 1966 and was a regular destination for educational trips with the high school for decades. In 2022, it was reopened and christened a museum of the future by the creative think tank and studio Next Nature. Founder and curator Koert Van Mensvoort fills the museum to the brim with sophisticated, future-exploring storylines in which the relationship between man, nature and technology is not only questioned, but also gently provoked from time to time. Next Nature is known for its very direct exhibits that can recognisably but intelligently charm a wide audience in the better search for the future.

- With their employment agency Hubot, Next Nature explored the future labour market when more and more professions are carried out in collaboration with robots.
- With their *Bistro In-vitro*, they explored the ethical boundaries of culinary creativity (from meat from the buttocks of well-known celebrities to mammoth meat) in a world where cultured meat is becoming the norm.
- I myself was once a guinea pig for their VR *Time machine*: a merry-go-round with VR glasses that treats us to an interstellar time travel.
- Because the Spacefarming exhibition reflects on what we are going to eat in space, and how we are going to produce it, it offers answers about what may end up on our plates in the near future here on Earth.

SPACESHIP EARTH

Most excitingly, Next Nature's explorations are keen to emancipate the integration of technology as an organic part of the natural world. The biosphere is the life support system of all living things, so human creativity and technological innovation should go hand in hand with ecological balance. That is the exciting co-evolution that Koert Van Mensvoort prefers to advocate. According to him, our image of nature as a separate world from technology is a convulsive and romantic fabrication. We should not go back to nature, but rather move forward with nature. And since time immemorial, technology has been our nature. Fortunately, because "there are no passengers on the spaceship Earth, we are all crew". It is a winged statement by Wubbo Ockels, after he was the first Dutch astronaut to set foot on the ground again in 1985. The metaphor of Earth as a spaceship was not new. In 1879, Henry George wrote in a novel about the earth as a "well-supplied ship, on which we sail through space". And in 1969, the American systems theorist and architect Richard Buckminster Fuller wrote his now legendary *Operation Manual for Spaceship Earth*. From that point of view, the Evoluon must be a docked training ship to provide the astronauts on spaceship Earth with an instruction manual for the 21st century, to train them and to encourage them to work together as a harmonious crew.

'There are no passengers
on the spaceship Earth.
We're all crew.'

———————

WUBBO OCKELS

NINE EXAMPLES OF
WONDER FROM BIODESIGN

We need to design more for nature,
with nature and like nature.

BRUSSELS AIRLINES | CACTUS LEATHER SHOES
FOR AIRLINE CREW

Gabrielle Szwarcenberg, a young member of the Antwerp Fashion Academy, designed the latest uniforms for the 2,600 pilots, airport staff and cabin crew of Brussels Airlines. The classic navy blue uniforms not only do away with traditional gender norms, they are also the result of close collaboration with Belgian clothing brands such as Ambiorix, Atelier Content and enjoyed valuable input from the staff on well-being in their unique work situation. Behind the timeless looks are creative design choices that have followed an ethical compass: cruelty-free wool and responsibly grown cotton became the minimum. Shoes were made from vegan leather based on grape and cacti, which was the first step of a high-quality piece of biodesign in a demanding application.

AGUAHOJA | NERI OXMAN STUDIO

Imagine if we could make materials, even entire buildings, grow and flourish with natural processes. Neri Oxman's five-metre-high sculpture is made entirely of cells from natural organisms and ushers in that thought with softness and beauty. It resembles a budding butterfly or an emerging leaf in spring, composed of 80% water and 20% biopolymers derived from trees, apples and shrimp. Inspired by shells and skins, the material was formed layer by layer into a biocomposite using a 3D printer. Biocomposites exhibit interesting properties such as insulation, moisture management and biodegradability. With the enchanting installation Aguahoja, Oxman shows that living materials and structures can respond positively to the environment: they can change shape, colour, rigidity, and organically disintegrate after use.

STELLA MCCARTNEY | REPLACING COTTON WITH KELP SEAWEED FIBRES

Organic, cruelty-free and fossil-free materials to replace leather, cotton and polyester are gaining momentum in the fashion industry and are gradually becoming super brands. Spiber™, Forager™, Mylo™, Bloom Foam™, Celium™, Ephea™, Airmycelium™ and many others are all manufactured in collaboration with little nature: bacteria, enzymes, fungi and algae. If you want to follow the rapid evolution, I would like to refer you to the Biofabricate Community led by Suzanne Lee, which unites the global frontrunners. To replace cotton and polyester, fashion designer Stella McCartey chooses Kelsun™, a material developed by Keel Labs from the fast-growing, renewable and regeneratively produced kelp seaweed. Kelsun clothing uses 70 times less water, gets rid of scarce land use, pesticides and has the potential to catapult the fashion industry a leap forward towards an ecologically responsible future. Its application in luxury brands promotes the credibility of biomanufacturing and pays tribute to the creative dance with nature.

KUKKA | COLOURING TEXTILES WITH DANCING BACTERIA

In a colourful manifesto of ecological rebellion, Dutch designers Laura Luchtman and Ilfa Siebenhaar show how they can colour environmentally friendly textiles with 'dancing' bacteria. Driven by the search for natural alternatives to the ecocide caused by the clothing sector with the dyeing of clothing, the designers unravelled the secret life of aerobic bacteria, which create a broad spectrum of pigments under the hypnotic sounds of sound waves. In the words of its designers, this bacterial paint factory offers a sustainable palette to embrace the world in vibrant colours without guilt. What can become a game changer for the entire fashion industry has been immortalised by Kukka in an open source book, so that not only her, but every inspired designer or brand can get to work with it.

In the fight against deforestation, researchers at MIT have developed a revolutionary method to generate woody plant material in the laboratory. By modifying chemicals during the growing process, they can precisely control the physical and mechanical properties of the resulting plant material. This means that they can 'grow' wooden products such as tables without cutting down trees, potentially significantly reducing the environmental impact. With the help of 3D bioprinting, they can grow plant material in shapes, sizes and structures that do not occur in nature.

ALGIX | BLOOM

In 2007, Ryan Hunt investigated how algae can be used to clean up harmful levels of phosphorus and ammonia in wastewater. However, after years of research, he discovered that the protein-rich algae biomass underwent a plasticisation process under heat, pressure and time. That was his 'aha' moment, after which he founded Algix. To show the world's manufacturers of footwear, sporting goods and accessories the versatility of its bio-based plastics, Algix launched the Vivobarefoot Bloom Ultra: a minimalist running shoe that is ultra-light, exceptionally resilient and moisture-absorbent. Today, Algix supplies a wide variety of bio-based algae-based plastics under the brand name Bloom to a variety of brands, where they are used in the soles of sports shoes, sports equipment and surfboards.

ECOLOGIC STUDIO | MERGING NATURE AND TECHNOLOGY IN BIODIGITAL SCULPTURES

After the growth structure of corals was translated into an algorithm that controls 3D printers, life-size sculptures were fabricated layer by layer that are reminiscent of alien trees and plants. The substrate has a texture of 4-millimetre triangular units called 'biopixels'. These are neatly arranged in a lattice of hexagons and provide space for one of the oldest organisms on earth: photosynthetic cyanobacteria, which convert sunlight into oxygen and biomass. The sculptures called H.O.R.T.U.S. XL want to help us question the increasingly blurred line between nature and technology.

Advertisers have always associated perfume with glamour and desire, but today a new story of unparalleled olfactory sensations is possible thanks to synthetic biology. In 2019, the collective Resurrecting the Sublime stunned with mystically scented installations at Centre Pompidou. Using DNA from extinct Hawaiian plants, enzymes were encoded that produced the same odours.

Using the discoveries of biotech company Ginkgo, fragrance artist Sissel Tolaas masterfully wove the scents of these flowers in her laboratory, using identical or similar scent molecules. Future Society similarly composed its perfume *Invisible Woods* from a flower that had become extinct due to drought in India in 1917. Perfume… Finally, there is a prospect of liberation from the predictable rule of celebrity ventures and duty-free aisles, and we can look forward to natural history time travel and other olfactory adventures.

WELOVEGLOWEE | LIGHTING STREETS WITH BIOLUMINESCENT BACTERIA

In the French town of Rambouillet, large glass cylinders rise up in the streets to replace street lamps. The French start-up WeLoveGlowee is experimenting with the bioluminescent, marine bacterium *Aliivibrio fischeri*, which stores solar energy in transparent piles filled with salt water during the day and releases it as light at night. Producing light with nature not only offers an energy-efficient future perspective, it also offers the prospect of night skies that are lit in a much more animal-friendly way. Before WeLoveGlowee found its way to many other places in France, even at the Roissy-Charles-de-Gaulle national airport, the story was translated into the educational exhibition *Biolumia*. It took place at one of Paris's most creative pop-up shops, Heureux les Curieux.

PROVOTYPING STEP 3

MAKING YOUR VISION VISIBLE WITH PROVOTYPING

Whether your provo type consists of an interactive installation in a shop, a sketch with actors in a market stall, or a fictional, but very realistic website, ... Provotyping most closely resembles theatre. In theatre, magic, light, sound, décor and acting are created in just a few square metres. One person can create a world in a square space with a few tables and chairs and the power of a good story that the audience is happy to be carried away in. Despite the fact that 'faking something' can feel uncomfortable for your team, provotyping is all about creating the right illusion.

'Provotyping means provocative prototyping:
we are going to gently violate people's idea of the future,
so that they open themselves up to new,
alternative futures.'

STEFAAN VANDIST

In addition to magic, it also has everything to do with eagerness to learn. With provotyping, I want to encourage people to make interventions that stimulate imagination and embrace new insights. But it runs in two directions. With a provo type, you also want to learn something from your audience. Not only do you want to get their 'feedback', but you also want to see their spontaneous and unfiltered 'authentic response': are they inspired? Do you see the light in their eyes? When do they get it? How do they share the experience with each other? How do they tell the tale?

INSIGHTS

What insights do I want to share with the audience?
And what do I want to learn from the audience?

When it comes to prototyping, the international innovation agency IDEO has the following wisdom: just as a picture is worth a thousand words, a good prototype is worth a thousand meetings.

Therefore, think with your team in terms of learning objectives, but in two directions: What insights do you want to share with the audience? But what would you like to learn from the audience by testing it out? Or because of what uncertainties are you going to experiment in the public space? Make two lists with your team to ultimately define two learning objectives on both sides.

EXPERIENCE

How can we creatively translate our vision of the future
into an interactive experience?

This stage requires a creative brainstorm where quantity is more important than quantity. Have your participants come up with as many ideas as possible individually. One idea per sticky note. You can boost the process with a collection of shining examples from many other sectors. Let participants briefly explain their ideas, make them clear and use the methodology of the decision tree to bring out the best ideas. The decision-maker can make a selection of the best ideas to advance to the next round.

STORY

Draw your provotyping idea into a visual story.

When we have selected one or more provotyping ideas and formats and are to implement them physically right away, we are bound to be delayed by a long chain of how- and why-questions. To avoid this, it is good to first translate your idea into a visual story.

Creating a cartoon or storyboard has its advantages:
- You're going to divide the whole provotyping experience linearly into steps: first this happens, and then that happens, ... This is what people see first, then people get to hear that, ...
- You draw it out from the visitor's point of view.
- You will come across numerous how-to questions: how do we lure people in? How do participants know that the experience is over? How do we make it easier for participants to convince their friends to join in? And so on...

By drawing the experience into a kind of comic strip, you are forced to take a critical look at each link. Moreover, this storyboard is an important foundation to create your provo type.

Have people individually create a storyboard in a grid of seven to twelve drawings. When people have to draw, nervousness always arises. Reassure them that they don't have to show any drawing talent. *'Ugly is ok'*, and stick guys are fine. When storyboards are ready, you can hold a small exhibition where stories are explained to each other. Participants can use sticky dots to indicate which stories they experience as the most powerful or even highlight parts that they find strong. Sometimes one storyboard clearly floats to the top, sometimes you can *'mix and match'* elements to something new under the guidance of the moderator.

PRODUCTION PLAN

Who and what do we need to build, execute,
and staff our provo type?

Finally, a production plan is needed. What materials, places, skills and people do we need? Not only to produce our provo type, but also during the period that our experience is operational for visitors? Who is going to observe and record how the general public experiences it?

OUR PROVOTYPING PROJECT

Write a teaser for your provotype project.

Write a short paragraph of text as if you were promoting a movie or theatre performance, but for your provo type. Also, give your provo type a name.

B-TONIC | A BETTER WORLD STARTS AT THE OFFICE

As a subsidiary of the Swiss insurer Baloise, B-Tonic is committed to improving well-being in the workplace. With their *People Sustainability Scan*, inspired by the Sustainable Development Goals (SDGs) and the Good Work Goals, B-Tonic identifies pain points, working points and formulates challenging goals.

Through provotyping, we create pilot projects together to test on the shop floor of customers. Think of meal boxes for shift workers to cook healthily for their families and office living rooms that bring homely cosiness and space for spontaneous and informal contacts to the office landscape.

GEMEENTE AMSTERDAM | CAR-FREE STREETS THANKS TO A POP-UP PARK

In 2023, Amsterdam underwent an intriguing design intervention. For six weeks, the municipality made a crucial access road to the city centre car-free. The first two days were tumultuous. However, local residents soon began to show appreciation. In fact, phase two consisted of the nightly installation of a real mobile pop-up park with trees on wheels. People got something in return to embrace. This intervention illustrates behavioural design at its best, according to behavioural designer Tom De Bruyne: disrupting one task (getting from A to B) and replacing it with a much more satisfying experience (my dead street becomes a lively park) produces advocates who transcend the predictable negative sentiment of the first few days. Making streets car-free with a pop-up park is now a common strategy in the Netherlands.

KINNARPS | THE PARK OFFICE
AND THE *MOST LOVED FURNITURE SHOP*

In a provotyping session with the Swedish office furnisher Kinnarps, the question was asked how we can develop the market for nature-inclusive office design. With pop-up offices in Belgian parks, people would be able to experience live what the gentle sensation of nature around you does to your mental well-being and work ethic. In addition, the strategic contours were determined for a second-hand shop made of Kinnarps furniture. As curators, well-known designers would combine daring furnishings with art and thus turn *preloved furniture into the most loved collections*. Kinnarps experienced how provotyping can get your teams to think out-of-the-box along the lines of ecological innovation perspectives.

NEW HEROES FOUNDATION |
POSSIBLE LANDSCAPES

After they built a life-size and itinerant demo house from mycelium and other biological materials with about one hundred and twenty organisations – to show that it is possible – the New Heroes Foundation focused on the Dutch landscape. How can we develop new, natural building materials in symbiosis with nature and the region? Their proposal for the Dutch pavilion for the World Expo in Osaka consisted of a walking park that represents the Netherlands and shows how the rich soil variation of the Netherlands can finally cut the umbilical cord between the construction sector and fossil raw materials. *Today, Possible landscapes* is mainly a roadshow to redo the exercise with various stakeholders, region by region: How is nature the main supplier for construction?

THE IMPETUS |
THE SUPERMARKET WITH REAL PRICES

A stone's throw from the Rijksmuseum of Amsterdam is a convenience store that at first glance seems normal. Only she charges her customers fair prices, or rather 'real prices'. In addition to the normal price, the price tags at the fruit and vegetable department also provide insight into social costs such as underpayment, land use, water use and climate impact. A bunch of bananas from Peru of 2.79 euros costs 2.94 euros after adding hidden costs. The provotyping stunt, initiated by Michel Scholte and his Impact Institute, was created to create support for the economic concept of *'True Cost Accounting'* and was followed by Deloitte, ABN Amro and Albert Heijn, among others, who are now also experimenting with it.

FRUITZ4LIFE | EDIBLE DEMONSTRATION LANDSCAPE

During a provotyping session with VogelaarVredehof, the exclusive supplier of top fruit at Albert Heijn, I enjoyed the enchanting décor of Fruitz4life, together with the team and colleague Jan Leyssens, which in itself can also be considered a provotype. In *agroforestry* , we produce food according to natural principles, but in human-designed food forests. For agricultural engineer Sjef Van Dongen, this scenario is all-encompassing: it offers young generations an attractive perspective in agriculture, promotes nature restoration, stimulates healthy local food and connects neighbourhoods with farmers. At Fruitz4life you will not only buy trees and shrub varieties for food forests, but you will also enter a demonstration landscape with boots to learn about design principles and business economics of *agroforestry*.

ELWOOD'S ORGANIC DOGFARM | ANIMAL-FRIENDLY DOG MEAT

When it comes to provotyping, it's okay to be a little cheeky. That's what they must have thought at Elwood's Organic Dogfarm when their dog meat was presented during a tasting at London's trendy Borough Market. Dogs are guaranteed to be organically bred, have enjoyed free range and are slaughtered in a humane manner. The tasting was what you can call a 'design performance' by animal rights activists. All the roasted meat was plant-based, but the story sent shockwaves through the audience. Provocation also makes you think: if we treated dogs and cats like chickens and pigs, we would immediately get prison sentences. So why do we treat farm animals and pets so differently?

111 jars of nail polish, 80 boxes of expired medicines, 1,000 children's books and comics, square metres full of electronics, cables, adaptors, remote controls, almost a tennis court of clothes on display... The television programme 'Sort Your Life Out' confronts families with their astronomical amount of – often unused – items in the house. An entire house is emptied and items are neatly arranged next to each other in a warehouse in different zones (clothing, decoration, bathroom items, etc.) The huge carpet of items is always a television sensation. Families can then decide what can be given away, recycled or reused in order to go home at least half lighter. Television, especially *docu-reality*, is often a source of inspiration for creative formats that can make complex problems very visible and tangible.

TERRA0 | SELF-MANAGING, AUTONOMOUS FORESTS

What if nature itself could autonomously decide how to offer its services?

Terra0, a Berlin-based experiment by artists and technologists, explores the possibility of an autonomous, technologically integrated and self-managing forest. Through sensors, IoT, and machine learning, this forest transacts, sells logging licences, monetises ecosystem services, accumulates capital, and acquires land, allowing it to expand autonomously. Terra0 is a *distributed autonomous organisation* (DAO) without a CEO but with an algorithm in charge. This experiment provokes our worldview, according to Jan-Peter Doomernik, innovation director at grid operator Enexis. Over coffee, we muse on questions such as: Can technology also enable autonomous energy infrastructure that is owned by the community? Can self-driving cars become a public service? And if technology merges with nature, will such autonomous structures ever become so cheap that market parties no longer see a business model in them?

'People don't know what they want
until you show them.'

———

STEVEN JOBS

PUBLIC SPACE: COMMERCIAL CENTRES 2.0

From 2021 to 2023, I found one of the most pleasant examples of a managed neighbourhood transformation on one of the busiest square kilometres in Western Europe. It enjoys Unesco status, but also the overwhelming presence of more than 3 million spectator, party, drug (and seesaw) tourists a year. I would like to take you to the Amsterdam district aka the Red Light District. *The Green Light District* was a particularly socially anchored initiative where policymakers, together with entrepreneurs and residents, transform the historic heart of Amsterdam into something new.

WELCOME TO THE GREEN LIGHT DISTRICT!

The mayor of Amsterdam, Femke Halsema, is well known to dare to think big. At odds with all the sailor romance, she is convinced that the future of prostitution should not lie in the historic heart of Amsterdam. To free the city centre from the nuisance, she wants a 'prostitution hotel plus' elsewhere in the city. Anyone who has also visited the Red Light District in 2022 in daylight could already notice a steady change. The Red Light District was subject to a silent takeover. Artists, designers, a new generation of catering operators and compact shops increasingly populated the tenement rooms with other pleasures.

If we can achieve a green transformation in the Red Light District with its specific social complexity, monumental buildings, and 17th-century canals, then it should succeed in every European historic city centre. "This could become a blueprint for any historic city," Thijs Reuten, chairman of The Green Light District, must have thought. Because of this potential, the European project Climate-KIC chose the Amsterdam Red Light District for a fascinating socio-cultural experiment: transforming the Red Light District into Green Canals. The European project Climate-KIC was an offensive to get ten European cities ahead of the crowd in order to achieve the status of circular and low-carbon city as early as 2030. They did this in cities such as Madrid, Copenhagen, but also in Amsterdam and Leuven by seeding innovative experiments, learning from them, and distributing those insights elsewhere in Europe. Climate-KIC is now Europe's most widely supported project on climate innovation.

When visiting The Green Light District, you will be taken along an alternative walk. The promenade leads you past green hotspots, hidden historical gems, cozy shops and idealistic eateries. On the menu you found Hempstory, Cacao & Spice, Latel, Eerlijk Waar, The Upcycle, De Prael, Condomerie, Ivy & Brös, Juice by Nature, Soepbar, Fashion for Good, … Everywhere you go, you'll be treated to a surprise.

One canal house from 1733 was given a major upgrade to become the most sustainable canal house in Amsterdam and was renamed The Green Light Hub. As a kind of green district house, it became the city living room and the central flywheel in the transformation of the Red Light District. Every student, designer or aspiring entrepreneur with a good idea for a Green Canal Belt could come here. After five weeks of coaching, your action or business plan came to fruition, and you were able to use the busy Green Light District as a testing ground and launch pad. Furthermore, residents, owners and entrepreneurs were taken by the hand through free intakes to energetically upgrade monumental buildings, shopping streets and residential blocks.

In the entire postcode area 1012, greening was literally initiated. Meetups and livestreams from green roofs explain to Amsterdammers how and why you could turn rooftops into climate gardens, how you could create breeding grounds for waterfowl in the canals themselves, create green banks and set up fish traps to fish plastic out of the canals. The Dutch 'tile flipping' championship generated a lot of enthusiasm and an accelerated spread of façade gardens and tree parks.

THE NEW COMMERCIAL CORE

So much for the transformation to hipster neighbourhood. But what about those other busy people-gathering places? What about our commercial centres, which show a high degree of predictability and vacancy everywhere in central cities? What about our Statiestraat, Dorpstraat or Nieuwstraat in a world of e-commerce and chains that offer the same everywhere? To start a brainstorming session, I present The Green Light District's approach to Stéphane Vanden Broeck of UNIZO, the largest membership organisation for independent entrepreneurs in Belgium. Stéphane has been supporting entrepreneurs, local trade associations and is passionate about regional, circular economy for many years. Stéphane is an infectious cross-thinker.

Stéphane is amused by the green ramparts and charmed by the social ap-proach, but does not believe in blueprints. The hipster mecca that The Green Light District is becoming is nice for the heart of Amsterdam and will be a good match with the type of tourists they would like to attract instead of drunken Brits, but every neighbourhood has a different DNA, a different dynamic, history, population composition and different needs. That's why you can never come up with a passe-partout solution and believe that it will be-come a success formula everywhere, says Stéphane. Since the rise of e-com-merce, but especially since the rise of shopping centres, home furnishing boulevards and retail outlets outside the city, you have to ask yourself wheth-er every central city needs an extensive commercial core or shopping street with the standard repertoire of retail brands at all. And above all: are they still economically feasible and realistic?

Street names in cities bear witness to a time when crafts were concentrated in neighbourhoods and where production and sales were not separated. As tech-nology enables quiet, safe and energy-efficient processes, commercial centres manufacturing industry can find its way back to the outskirts of the city and even reappear on the shop floor. But in addition to technology, new consumer trends are also driving the way. The young Generation Z (people born between 1995 and 2010) smashes much more of their budget in the hospitality industry than the over-40s, but is looking for affordable, convenience-oriented and righteous con-cepts such as the spaghetti restaurant Bavet for example, according to Stéphane.

'The current retail model
of "more of the same for less"
needs to be replaced by "less but better".'

STÉPHANE VANDEN BROECK

"If we look globally, the current retail model of 'more of the same for less' should be tilted to a model of 'less but better'. But we will have to make that visible and tangible locally again. Because we don't know what we want until we see it." Examples include:

- Once a run-down, covered shopping arcade, Brixton Village in London is now the most vibrant place for foodies thanks to more than 100 entrepreneurs from 50 nationalities who have created a melting pot of unpretentious restaurants with an Afro-Caribbean vibe.

- ReTuna, Sweden's first-ever shopping mall with second-hand clothing and goods, provides a glimpse into how recycling parks, thrift stores and shopping streets can merge into new maker districts and fashion avenues based on reuse.
- *Thanks* to a young, strong traders' association, the Bergstraat in Heist-op-den-berg has managed to develop a beautiful cluster of beauty, wellness and health. But their fight for the core also ensures that well-known names can be found in that core and not in a track shopping complex.
- *Curated* by Edo is the successor of Edo Collective in Antwerp and shows a nice mix of sustainable brands. They also provide the platform and a face to new makers and products. In this way, they really bring the identity of their suppliers into the store as a fully-fledged experience.
- *Lutgart* is a hothouse for young entrepreneurs who promote their new products to the local population with a summer bar, city beaches and other city events. After three schools merged into one campus in the Limburg city of Beringen, the vacant buildings were used as a campus for local and starting entrepreneurial talent. Affordable space is offered to a new generation of entrepreneurs who can develop their offerings there.

New commercial centres should have their own soul and unique DNA based on the needs that manifest themselves, the people who live there and the entrepreneurs who are there. And there are certainly examples that show municipal authorities that this is possible. What needs to be completely overhauled are the standard solutions where urban blighters are given a residential or retail real estate project that no one was waiting for, according to Stéphane. More and more entrepreneurs in such a commercial centre are also calling attention to resting places, green oases. They also innovate in bringing their idea to fruition. For example, a start-up entrepreneur came up with his business plan by asking the neighbourhood what they needed. It turned out to be a coffee bar. Not shockingly innovative, but the way in which it is done all the more. Municipalities experience competitive pressure from each other and far too often follow a 'placemaking theory' in which economic policy is not in line with social needs. We should embrace an urban blight as a godsend in order to breathe life into local economy projects that nourish and strengthen the existing social fabric. According to Stéphane, it is up to cities and municipalities to change the context. They draw up a policy. And policy means society.

*'It's up to the municipal authorities.
They draw up the policy.
Policy means society.'*

———————

STÉPHANE VANDEN BROECK

Of course, you also need strong holders for that. I live in Edegem, a few minutes by bike from the Statielei in the Antwerp suburb of Mortsel. In this street, in addition to vacancy, a lot of faded glory and the usual chains, you also have a number of young entrepreneurs with strong store concepts that are quite popular. I can still see the people behind César (men's clothing), Plume (interior items), zwArt (drawing materials), Rand (ecological clothing) and Granelle (packaging-free store) putting their shoulders to the wheel of initiatives that bring the entire shopping street towards a turnaround. It would be good to instrumentalise trade associations with the necessary tools to put pressure on their policymakers. The oversized database of the Public Space Information Point, which is chock-full of inspiration and tools for architects, urban planners and policymakers, would be a good weapon depot for this.

A VISION LIBRARY FOR THE SHOPPING STREET

A creative approach was developed by Pantopicon – a studio for exploration and design – for the municipality of Meerssen, located near the city of Maastricht. An empty shop building was transformed into an inspiring space, filled with ideas for alternative uses for shop premises. Instead of clothes hangers with trousers and camisoles, there were coat racks with graphics and descriptions of some sixty unique concepts, such as co-hotels in historic buildings, tea rooms where you can consult regional care services, and test kitchens where a different chef cooks every week.

Hundreds of visitors a day wandered through the various alternative ideas for the shopping street. They were then invited to choose their own favourite 'ensemble' and discuss it with the moderators. With the vision library, the municipal administration was able to enter into dialogue with its residents in an intuitive and constructive way in order to understand the real needs that do not necessarily have to be met with traditional retail chains.

British retail guru Ibrahim Ibrahim divides the current retail landscape into four mental spaces. With some overlap, there is everything that people appreciate because it is 'fast' (quick choice, ordering and receiving at home, etc.) versus everything that is appreciated because it is deliberately slow (experience, relaxation, meeting, enjoyment, learning, etc.). Next, entrepreneurs with a physical retail space need to think carefully about what they want from people: Do you want people to buy your brand? Or do you want them to join your brand? The traditional set-up, in which a physical store is a stock with a cash register where turnover per square metre is the measure of success, is tenable for fewer and fewer traders. To keep your shopping experience healthy, ideas, surprise, sensation, happiness, engagement and experiences to be shared per square metre, per month or per year are at least as important a measure.

A 'what if' question that I have asked many a city council is: "What if your shopping street was a music festival? And what if your entrepreneurs are the pop stars there? What would be on the bill?" By asking that question, you help those involved out of the traditional idea that shopping streets are the sum of shops in a row, and you open up a spectrum of experiential strategies to achieve a distinctive character and appeal of your shopping neighbourhood.

NINE GREAT EXAMPLES TO IMPROVE THE BUILT ENVIRONMENT

NEW WEST END COMPANY | SMART STREET

How can we show our vision of tomorrow's trading core today?

After London Mayor Sadiq Aman Khan had taken a bulk package of measures against air pollution in 2016 (from low emission zones to measures to promote bicycle traffic and multimodal transport), he wanted to create an attractive prospect of car-free shopping streets. Bird Street, a side street of Oxford Street, became an experience zone of the 'smart street': a shopping promenade with art, greenery and air-purifying technology incorporated into street furniture. Stepping stones provided kinetic energy. It was one of the earliest examples of provotyping in the public space that my colleague Herman Konings and I visited. The Smart Street conveyed the vision for the future of the shopping street of trade association New West End Company together with a broad coalition of traders, urban planners and tech companies.

THE CAIRO PROBIOTIC TOWER | AN URBAN ECO-POWERHOUSE

What if we merge nature and industry in the city?

The planned Probiotic Tower in Cairo can be seen as a living, breathing creature that enters into a symbiotic relationship with its challenging, urban environment. At the heart of this ecological powerhouse is an oversized algae bioreactor that converts CO_2 into biofuel and provides potable water for neighbouring residential areas. The upper floors are occupied by a bamboo plantation, the wood of which is locally processed into industrial cross-laminated timber for the surrounding house construction. Furthermore, algae and photovoltaic panels on the façades provide a multiplier effect of its positive impact. It is the holistic blueprint that provides answers to ecological challenges in metropolises in the south, which earned it the Future Project of the Year Award 2023 at the World Architecture Festival.

LOLA LANDSCAPE ARCHITECTS | THE REWILDING OF AMSTERDAM AIRPORT SCHIPHOL

How can we even connect an airport with natural values?

After Schiphol Group approached the design studio LOLA to explore long-term developments, LOLA proposed a series of radical approaches in which biodiversity is a prerequisite for a more sustainable airport. Instead of seeing birds as a safety risk, LOLA advocated a strategy of landscape restoration with more forests, taller grass, ecological management and rewilding to encourage at-risk species to migrate to other places. Schiphol could then evolve from a scarecrow to a bird sanctuary.

We looked at the airports of Munich, Frankfurt and Oslo, which also have a spatial connection to nature. Nature would also be measurably used to purify air from particulate matter, dampen noise, temper heat and reduce stress among travellers.

HKRITA | ROBOTIC PRODUCTION THEATRE

What if automation brought manufacturing back within the city limits?

How can new high street experiences engage consumers with hopeful perspectives? The fashion world, which is so often shrouded in a haze of shine and glitter, hides a dark reality of pollution and waste. In this shadowy reality, there are several glimmers of hope, including the clothing-2-clothing microtheatre of HKRITA from Hong Kong. Like a magic box, this twelve-metre-long shipping container reveals the secret of sustainable fashion. Consumers bring in old garments, after which they witness a magical metabolism and seven-step process, from cleaning to manufacturing brand-new textiles through digital knitting techniques. It's not just a recycling process; it is magical production theatre that offers the spectator a glimpse of a distributed and locally realised sustainable future for the fashion industry. The machine is a basis for circular material cycles.

*How can we close material and goods flows
at neighbourhood level?*

In order to visualise a future in which the flow of goods finds their way
through our environment in a much more intelligent way, the Swedish fintech
company Klarna has developed a contemporary, digital version of a relic that
is easy to ignore: the letterbox. Their modular mailbox is a *community locker*
for the neighbourhood with compartments to receive parcels and groceries,
a recycling module to process packaging into new raw materials, a sharing
compartment to share things with your neighbours and a built-in 3D printer.
The aim of the speculative design is to get project developers, e-commerce
companies, transport companies and city councils around the table to think
together about more efficient city logistics.

LOCHAL TILBURG | THE CITY LIVING ROOM

*What if cities and municipalities offered a town hall room
for their residents?*

Today, two former railway sheds house various local associations: the library,
meeting places, theatre stages, an atrium, restaurant, coffee bar, exhibition
space, co-working, a time lab, a food lab, a digilab, a future lab, a word lab, a
game lab and much more. In addition to this accumulation of hip and contemporary forms to bring people together, something else stands out. LocHal
invites you to lose yourself in the human habitat all day long. Despite its
robust, industrial character, it is home to an archipelago full of cosy and cosy
corners and places that invite you to meet. LocHal in Tilburg was voted World
Building of the Year in 2019.

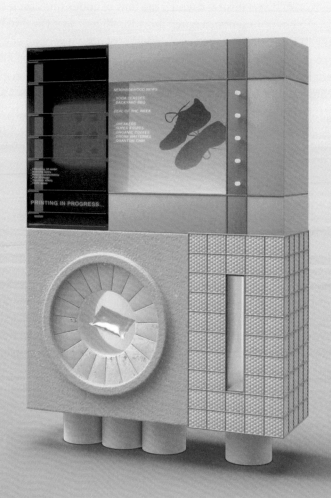

What if we made a few percent of our open space edible?

What if 5% of Flanders' agricultural land, private gardens, public domain, industrial sites and schoolyards had a food forest character? In one fell swoop, we would generate 20% extra food through a new form of agriculture that we can call 'experiential agriculture' and is part of the public space. Louis De Jaegher, Belgium's most renowned food forest designer, has developed a plan for the Department of Agriculture and Fisheries, with the aim of providing Flanders with an infrastructure for basic food production and how it can be managed with pleasure and dedication by the citizen. One of the strengths of a food forest is its great feasibility.

STREET MOVES | YOUR STREET BACK ON A HUMAN SCALE THANKS TO A CONSTRUCTION KIT

What if car-free neighbourhoods lead to new types of urban furniture?

The think tank ArkDes and design agency Vinnova have created a kit for urban furniture, with which they want to create a one-minute city. Here, it's all about the immediate space as soon as you step out your front door. Street Moves aims to transform the streetscape into a social space as before, before it was dominated by traffic fixtures. In seven Swedish cities, including Stockholm, grey parking lanes are being transformed into lively ribbons with picnic furniture, terrace tables, benches, green spaces, neighbourhood vegetable gardens, fountains, bicycle and shared scooter parking facilities, playgrounds and charging stations. The modules, inspired by Ikea, Lego and Minecraft, allow local residents to design the urban environment themselves, after which they are delivered to the neighbourhood as a kit.

NUDES | GREEN UPGRADES TO THE CITY

*What if green infrastructure is made possible
with modular architecture?*

NUDes stands for Natural and Urban Devices. Architect Jose Maria Mateo
Torres developed these modular 'extension sets' for the city as living gems to
quickly add green spaces to commercial buildings, homes and streets. His collection consists of extension systems to make trees show off on balconies, to
expand façades with vertical urban vegetable gardens or to transform parking
spaces into beautiful mini gardens in no time.

THE NEW BAUHAUS MOVEMENT |
HOW DO YOU BUILD A NEW EUROPE?

How can we get an entire continent moving to reinvent itself?

The European Green Deal should not just be a legal framework imposed
from above. That is why substantial investments are being made in a base
of more than 100,000 organisations that together are called the New European Bauhaus Movement. This movement aims to bring together the power
of imagination and new planning ideas among educators, scientists, technologists, architects and artists. This is the only way Europe can become a
planetary laboratory for the future, according to captain Franscesca Bria. She
likes to refer to the city of Barcelona, which managed to thin out 60% of car
ownership thanks to interventions in the urban structure. For her, open data
platforms have a key role to play, and it is crucial that they are developed as a
public infrastructure.

'The walkable city
is the city of the future.
It promotes health, sustainability
and social cohesion,
and it provides space
for creativity and innovation.'

———

JEFF SPECK,
URBAN PLANNER AND AUTHOR

CELEBRATION

5
CELEBRATION

——

In a communications universe where the future is often trapped in doomsday scenarios, outdated legislation, dry reports and technical terms, there is a liberating approach: celebrate. Celebrating new insights and breakthroughs through provo-typing shines a light on the way forward. As soon as there is something to celebrate, everyone likes to come and be under the spotlight. Celebration resonates deep in our hearts, so you'd better make sure the most impactful projects get their deserved applause.

EVENTS: THE MUSIC FESTIVAL AS A LIVING LAB FOR THE WORLD

During a walk in the park in corona time, I had my first meeting with Joris Beckers – the driving force behind Love Tomorrow. During that conversation, it dawned on me that a music festival is a temporary micro-society where you can experiment with the future without limits. A festival is a pop-up city where we are housed together with tens of thousands of people in a tempo-rary setting, wake up, want to move freely, brush our teeth, take a shower, are hungry all at the same time, need to hydrate ourselves all day, where we appreciate a clean toilet, ... And all these actions should not frustrate the overall experience, but should enrich it, according to Joris. A festival visit offers an escape from the everyday and enters a new world where our senses are sharpened. We eagerly let every sensation come in. This offers unique opportunities to address people's behaviour and worldview as well.

Love Tomorrow is the organisation that lent its name to the future conference of the same name on the hallowed ground of Tomorrowland. But above all, it is the team behind the experiential sustainability interventions on the festival site and its Dreamville campsite.

Greening a festival, ... This involves a mobility plan in which various municipalities and institutions are involved, large-scale operations on food supply, waste management, an intensive consultation and participation process with the neighbourhood, a water and energy plan, care for nature on the site, but also the development of positive experiences in which behaviour is consciously but often unconsciously controlled. The great thing is that the context of a festival offers many more opportunities than 'greening the festival'. Many of the social and ecological challenges that are insidiously manifesting themselves in society, but increasingly loudly, are extremely directly visible and tangible in the context of a festival. Its flexibility, temporary set-up, creative culture and large audience make it the ideal setting to test the solutions that the future desperately needs on the hundreds of thousands of guinea pigs who unleash their inner child every year.

'Festivals are laboratories for testing and learning, mini-cities that serve as catalysts for circularity in urban systems and stages to inspire and engage others.'

———————

TIJL COUZIJ, *INTO THE GREAT WIDE OPEN*

FOR THE LOVE OF TOMORROW

And then there's the enormous sonic power of festivals. Literally and figuratively. Why wait until your festival is 100% green, climate neutral or has the status of circular or regenerative before you play your best cards?

In 2022, Love Tomorrow, G-Stic (organiser of international innovation conferences) and Vito (Flemish Institute for Technological Research) joined forces to organise a festival for the future on the hallowed ground of Tomorrowland. In this way, the sound power of Tomorrowland and its fairytale terrain can be used to inspire us with the greatest adventure of our time: the transformation to a future-proof society. As co-curator of Love Tomorrow 2022, 2023 and 2024, it was a privilege for me to put many of my personal heroes such as Barbara Belvisi, Leen Gorissen, Nadine Bongaerts, Lucas De Man, Dennis Karpes, Yuval Noah Harari and Rutger Bregman, their vision and projects in the spotlight. As Rutger Bregman would put it: the biggest source of waste is talent. And if there's one place where there's a lot of talent to be found, it's Tomorrowland: it shows us how to inspire and move a mass of people. In that light, we had better use the best of ourselves by offering international vision-aries and future makers – aka the creators of tomorrow – the biggest stage for the wonder of society.

Our speaker briefing reflects the idea of provotyping. We ask everyone on stage to tell a story that posits an attractive perspective for progress. We also ask them to inspire the audience on how they can join in. But the most impor-tant criterion for bringing someone's story to the stage is that they generously share with us how they make their vision visible and tangible with 'boots on the ground'.

A FESTIVAL AS A TESTING GROUND FOR THE WORLD

Paradise City, in the Flemish Brabant town of Perk, has been among the world's top greenest festivals since it was twice awarded the highest possible rating by 'A Greener Festival', an independent, internationally recognised NGO.

The appreciation goes out to the pioneering role. In addition to zero tolerance for disposable cups and packaging, a 100% vegetarian menu and composting toilets, a partnership with Eneco provides a Green Power Plan. With solar islands, battery containers and green electricity, they want to move to 100% electricity from renewable sources by 2025. The construction of the festival is also done with solar energy, a first in the Belgian event industry. The immense ecological footprint of mobility is dealt with as much as possible with night trains and shuttle buses to train stations in order to relieve the festival and surrounding access roads of car traffic as much as possible.

The Dutch festival DGTL focuses mainly on circularity, picking up on the policy framework of its home city of Amsterdam, which has the ambition to become a circular city by 2050. By 2030, Amsterdam wants to reduce its incoming material flows by half compared to 2021. The City of Amsterdam is inspired by Oxford economist Kate Raworth's Doughnut model and wants to become a Doughnut city. Xander Kotvis, revolution manager at Apenkooi (the organisation behind DGTL) designed the Material Flow Index to make DGTL a first Doughnut festival. DGTL is now a data-driven circular festival where incoming and outgoing material and energy flows are closely monitored and where suppliers are encouraged to push their boundaries. Zap Concepts was commissioned to design a smart grid to steer DGTL away from diesel generators and run on 100% renewable energy. The site of the former Dutch Dock and Shipbuilding Company (NDSM) is now equipped with an arsenal of solar panels that ensures that the festival site produces more energy than it consumes on an annual basis.

Daniela Berenguer researched at Radboud University (Nijmegen, the Netherlands) how the festival scene can contribute to circular and climate-neutral regions, cities and neighbourhoods and came up with a list of solutions that can have a positive impact on urban systems. She purposefully talks about 'solutions', because she also identified a concern: when we talk about the future, we often have tunnel vision towards innovation, and then we risk spreading limited resources very thinly. Fortunately, there is consensus within the Dutch 'Green Deal Circular Festivals' that it makes much more sense to make existing – new and old – solutions accessible, to make them known, to connect them with each other and to explore the possibilities of them in vivo in the field so that everyone experiences how it can work.

Seven shining examples of how the festival can be the testing ground for the world:
- To challenge the excessive use of polystyrene foam in set construction, set builder Simon Carroll developed the spiral-shaped, demountable and easily upgradeable Hayes Pavilion for the Glastonbury Festival. In this way, he shows the world the technical and aesthetic possibilities with recycled wood and mycelium.
- Shambala's *festival* in the UK has been the testing ground in the development of the Green Event Code, which aims to develop common standards for events across the UK.
- Greener is a mobile battery solution that has been extensively tested and perfected in the festival industry and has since been used more widely in all industries where mobile energy plays a key role in the energy transition: think of construction, road works, housing, transport, solar parks, etc.

- Waterville is a living laboratory of Love Tomorrow in collaboration with VITO and the University of Antwerp that promotes smart water use at events and cities thanks to smart networks (an internet-of-water) and life monitoring of water consumption patterns. The Waterbar by the Belgian cleantech company Bosaq adds the magic of locally extracting water and upcycling it into drinking water and presenting it as a total experience.
- Turn Systems is a logistical system to distribute reusable cups and, above all, to have them returned via an electronic reward system without having to pay a deposit. Live Nation believes it can achieve up to 90% return rate at events such as Lollapalooza and wants to increase this further.
- Earth Today helps the Lowlands festival to protect up to 60,000 m^2 of nature. That's 1 m^2 per Lowlander. Together, they want to create a new kind of Live Aid that offers the general public an action perspective to contribute to nature. By 2050, half of the planet's nature should be protected.
- *The circular Foodcourt* is a concept of the sustainable festival facilitator Revolution Foundation to combat food loss and packaging waste in festival catering. At Elrow Town Amsterdam, for example, the focus is on plant-based menus, composting of waste, hard cup systems, recycling points, behavioural design and a connection with a general raw materials plan for the entire festival.

Modular structures, regenerative design, circular principles, design, material and energy flows inspired by nature... My hope is that in the coming years we will see more and more bold experiments on festival grounds. We don't have to limit ourselves to architecture and engineering, but we will certainly continue to explore the potential of behavioural design. How can we create interventions full of experience and experimentation that teach us all kinds of things about human behaviour?

Have you been to the Efteling theme park as a child, parent or grandparent? Then you have undoubtedly seen Holle Bolle Gijs. Holle Bolle Gijs is a full-figured fairytale character who has taken post in various places between the attractions and shouts 'paper here'. Visitors of all ages have traditionally happily shoved packaging waste from ice creams, snacks and soft drink cups into his mouth and were invariably treated to acknowledgments and accolades for their environmentally conscious behaviour.

Holle Bolle Gijs is an early and legendary example of behavioural design, more specifically of the psychological technique of *feedback reinforcement*. Correct behaviour is then immediately rewarded with a positive experience. Instead of informing or teaching people with communication, education or signage, we create interventions in behavioural design that intuitively encourage people to behave in the desired way. After all, more than 80% of our behaviour is unconscious, routine and driven by emotions. That means that less than 20% of our behaviour is the result of rational and conscious choices. In line with Daniel Kahneman's book *Thinking, Fast & Slow*, 2011, behavioural designers distinguish between the rational, reflective system of the brain (also called the Dr. Spock brain) and the intuitive and impulsive system (also called the Homer Simpson brain). When we know how to manipulate the Homer Simpson brain by discouraging undesirable behaviour and stimulating desired behaviour, we can often control people's behaviour much more effectively than with communication that has to pass through the rational brain.

FESTIVALS AS SACRED GROUND
FOR CONTEXT CREATION

The last example shows that behavioural design is always part of a communication frame and a worldview. You can see behavioural change and influencing perception and opinion separately from each other. Whereas behavioural design often focuses on how our brain works, context design is often focused on the interplay of social actors such as industry, government, academics and the general public. Context design aims to show the world that it can be done, and in doing so, to increase pressure and shift the social norm. What seems bizarre, unrealistic and exceptional today must be made normal and commonplace.

Four examples of behaviour design during live events:

- *Feedback reinforcement* can also be found in the kinetic dancefloor that has been used at Coldplay concerts, among others. The more violently concertgoers dance, the more kinetic energy is produced by the system under the floor tiles. This is also made visible with animations. Society as a whole has to go through an energy transition, but most people among us hardly know what a kiloWatt-hour is... Interventions such as these will adjust this through playful experiences.

- *Option reduction* is a very effective technique for controlling behaviour. It simply consists of channel the supply to options that are desired. In collaboration with Beyond Meat, DGTL has been a vegan festival since 2014. The only burgers are Beyond burgers with which they do not so much want to appeal to the vegan, but to surprise and please the much more numerous '*conflicted carnists*' with a plant-based alternative.

- *Creating friction* is also a fun technique. Can we remove obstacles or add them to motivate the right behaviour? Mobility is the elephant in the room at almost all events. The biggest environmental impact is determined by artists, employees and the public who move around. That is why the sustainable event agency Utopia invariably chooses locations that are located a lazy stone's throw from a large train station. That is precisely why the Om Conference marketing conference is being organised in the Queen Elisabeth Hall, next to Antwerp Central Station. You must be al little stupid to get to the centre of Antwerp by car.

- *Hyperbolic discounting* means that our brain perceives risks in the distant future as smaller than risks that manifest themselves in the here and now. Reason enough to use the power of creativity and live entertainment to bring those risks to the present. That's what the Dutch artist and tech poet Daan Roosegaarde did with his manifestation Waterlicht. At a series of iconic places in Europe, he used a light show to show how the world would change with rising sea levels. It was a numinous and magical experience, but one that made large masses of people realise that the world is changing.

Some examples of interventions at festivals that can lead to new social norms and even new policies:

- With her coalition of the willing around reusable cups, Billie Cups showed the world that you can make a festival like the Gentse Feesten run entirely on reusable cups. It led to one of the earliest and most progressive laws on single-use packaging at events in the EU.
- A sore point at international festivals is air travel. SkyNRG, the producer of the so-called SAF (Sustainable Aviation Fuel based on algae or frying oil) works together with international festivals to make their air traffic more sustainable. From 2015 onwards, airlines will be obliged to dilute their fuels by 2% with SAF. Jef De Vries, programme manager at SkyNRG, wants to increase the pressure by having well-known artists fly at 20% SAF in the eyes of the general public. In this way, he wants to show that both the legislator and the industry can be much more ambitious.
- At DGTL, SeMiLLA Sanitation was allowed to work with its space technology to process human urine into pure water and nutrients that can be used to grow food. This led to the playful project *'pee to tea'* where fresh peppermint was grown on the residue from our lake. For example, DGTL played a key role in the development of technology that will further prove its usefulness in urban but also humanitarian applications such as in refugee camps where rapid response and construction of temporary infrastructure is crucial. In an interview, CEO Peter Scheer also indicates that he wants to put pressure on governments. Today, it is forbidden to use raw materials from human excrement in food production, which is a serious obstacle to the development of many circular and decentralised food systems.
- Since 2021, the Lowlands car parks have been home to the largest solar carport in the world. As many as 90,000 photovoltaic panels form a roof for parked cars. Together with Lowlands, Novar realised this enormous solar roof to show the various advantages of it and to show that it is possible. The new environmental law in the Netherlands of 2023 provides that parking lots from a certain size must also be equipped with a solar roof.

THE SOCIAL DIMENSION AS MY OWN BLIND SPOT

Festivals and events are the ultimate medium to experiment with the solutions to tomorrow's challenges. Through interventions such as provotyping, you can make a new world visible and tangible. While writing this story, I was allowed to give a keynote about it during the annual Echo24 event of the Belgian event sector, which on February 6, 2024 was all about sustainable events. With fresh research, I made a plea for provotyping, for the greening of festivals, but also to open festivals as much as possible for the demonstration of sustainable concepts, research and experimentation. I also caught myself in a blind spot, and it was social. The elephant in the room during the whole conference was not mobility or air travel, as I would imagine, but the status of employees. During heated panel discussions, words such as exploitation of volunteers or 'social fraud' were not shunned. So it's high time to shine a new light on that as well and – who knows – to come to a new balance by experimenting with new forms of cooperation.

PROVOTYPING
STEP 4
CELEBRATION - CELEBRATE EVERY BREAKTHROUGH WITH EVERYONE

Across history, cultures and generations, celebration functions as the yarn that binds the fabric of society. From ancient rituals to modern festivities, celebrations fulfil fundamental psychological needs by providing moments of relief from the mundane, opportunities for self-expression, and opportunities for social interaction. They nourish the human spirit and provide nourishment for the soul. They are the mirrors that reflect the values, beliefs and aspirations of a society and the vehicles by which cultural identity and values are transmitted from one generation to the next. So much for this ratatouille of pompous statements by well-known anthropologists, sociologists and historians who try to grasp the intrinsic value and meaning of celebrations.

 With provotyping, you shine new light on the future and create new perspectives around which you can bring people together. By integrating the codes of celebrations into a communication universe where the future is often trapped in doomsday scenarios, outdated legislation, dry reports and technical terms, there is a liberating approach: celebrate. Celebrating new insights and breakthroughs through provotyping shines a light on the way forward. As soon as there is something to celebrate, everyone likes to come and be under the spotlight. Celebration resonates deep in our hearts, so you'd better make sure the most impactful projects get their deserved applause.

COMMUNICATION OBJECTIVES

What do you want people to say to each other
after experiencing the provo type?

Who and what exactly do we want to achieve with our provo type? Do we want to promote a new innovation perspective? Do we want to change a false perception? Or do we want to collect new wishes from the public? Formulate what makes you evaluate the entire provotyping operation as a valuable intervention.

PUBLIC

What is your target audience and what action do you
expect from them?

How can we describe our target group and, above all, what views, doubts or uncertainties exist around the themes we provopose? And how can we reach and touch them? But also: What actions do we expect from them? Does the experience provide them with interaction or dialogue? Do we want them to share their experiences and new questions with us? Do we want them to share their experience with others?

CONTEXT

In which setting will your provo type be most relevant?

Do you need an empty commercial building in a shopping street to survey residents in your municipality? Or are you better off looking for a place at a trade fair or conference to reach people in a specific sector? Choose a place, period and medium for your provo type that fits your target audience and goals.

ROADMAP

*How do we get everything produced,
executed and evaluated in 100 days?*

When you ask participants to make a 100-day plan, you can feel the atmosphere in a team change. The conceptual and strategic mode immediately shifts into planning. Even though it's pretty much the same, a hundred days sounds more urgent than three months. In a 100-day plan, tomorrow is the first day, and each day is crossed out. From now on, we will no longer think but *think ahead*: we will script the whole story ahead of how we can create, plan, market, operationalise, and execute the provo type as a team week after week in 100 days. What are the key moments? Where and when will the provo type be launched? What is the role of our partners in the coalition of the willing? Does it take a route to other places? How do we connect to other events? Where and how are results shared and celebrated?

CELEBRATION

*How can we celebrate our vision of the future
with our provo type?*

This is perhaps the final question. When we talk about the future, we often don't know what we want. We often don't believe what's possible until we see it, or even better: until we experience the future. With provotyping, we can tackle the crisis of imagination by involving people in an intervention that can make you feel a touch of wonder.

NEW ZEALAND | GARBAGE CANS WITH GOLD STARS

How can we celebrate good sorting behaviour?

Inspired by pedagogical reward systems for pre-school children, the New Zealand city of Christchurch introduced a system in which families who sort well are given a large, visible gold star on their wheelie bin. After the corona crisis, the percentage of waste delivered that was correctly sorted for recycling dropped to 48%. People who did not sort correctly up to three times received learning notifications that were visibly affixed to their container. The reward system, in combination with the sanctioning of persistent 'slant-sorters', managed to increase the percentage to no less than 80% in just a few months.

FUTERRA | THE IRRESISTIBLE GOALS
FOR THE ANTHROPOCENE BY 2050

How can we finally captivate creatives with the SDGs?

The United Nations Sustainable Development Goals (SDGs) for 2030 may have acquired the status of the Twelve Commandments among international institutions and policymakers, but … They don't resonate very much among creatives. A pity, because the future is full of design tasks and creative challenges. That's why the British creative agency Futerra wondered aloud: "What if we have the SDGs behind us by the year 2030?" And then launched 'The 2050 Awesome Anthropocene Goals'. Are you also convinced that gender should be a source of joy? Do you agree that by 2050 all consumption should be regenerative? Or do we go for 100 terrawatts of renewable energy as a human right? Indulge in goals that are irresistible and invite you to celebrate a creative feast around them.

SUPERKILEN PARK |
GENEROSITY AS A DESIGN GOAL

*How can we practise a city's diversity and implicit richness
on a daily basis?*

Superkilen Park in Nørrebro, the most diverse district in Copenhagen, is de-signed so that cultural differences cheerfully chafe and reveal their richness. The Danish architectural firm BIG brings newcomers and locals together on the square with a mix of street furniture from different cultures, including Finnish bicycle parking, Belgian benches, a Moroccan water feature, Iraqi swings and as many as sixty artifacts from various cultures. To this end, BIG worked together with local residents. Superkilen Park is a lively place with a weekly market and celebrates life during the summer with board games and a sports and relaxation zone under Japanese cherry and Lebanese cedar trees.

MASTERCARD | USING BIG DATA
FOR THE INTEGRATION OF REFUGEES

*How do you celebrate the power of technology
for humanitarian challenges?*

One month after Russia's invasion of Ukraine, a quarter of the population was already on the run. 10 million refugees crossed the border into Poland and 1.5 million stayed there for a long time. With those numbers, a humanitarian crisis quickly becomes a housing crisis and an employment crisis. In Warsaw, rents skyrocketed and the labour market was under a lot of pressure. Based on Mastercard's vast mountain of transactional data, it turned out that small-er Polish cities had much more to offer in terms of accommodation, infra-structure and employment. That's why Mastercard developed the *wheretoset-tle* platform based on cross-links between its own data and that of the Polish Central Statistical Office and a series of real estate and job portals. If properly distributed, it soon became clear that Poles were not only helping Ukrainian refugees, but also the other way around. Local aldermen and mayors started promoting their own city as a destination. 20% of Ukrainian refugees in Po-land used wheretosettle to find a place and a job in their new host country.

How do you celebrate the process of sustainable innovations instead of the final destination?

The most talked about sustainability communication of 2023 is without a doubt '*Mother Nature needs a status report*' by computer giant Apple. In this video, Mother Nature – played by Oscar-winner Octavia Spencer – demands accountability from Apple's environmental experts. They are clearly under pressure to impress with innovations in materials, clean energy, low-carbon shopping experience and the restoration of natural ecosystems. Mother Nature, strict and demanding, braces herself to be disappointed but ultimately gives Apple the benefit of the doubt. With a lot of self-awareness, Apple shows that there is still a lot of work to be done, but also shows that it is better to celebrate your incomplete process imperfectly and vulnerably than your far-away vague sustainability goals.

BREWDOG | WE CAN'T WAIT FOR NORTH KOREA

How Brewdog celebrates its ethical values by challenging the status quo.

The Scottish regenerative beer brand Brewdog brews its beer on stale bread and offsets its CO_2 emissions twice by funding nature restoration in the Scottish Highlands. Her communication style is that of a brutal Tijl Uilenspiegel who goes to war against injustice. During the World Cup, it shamed other beer brands by profiling itself as an anti-sponsor: "*First Russia, then Qatar, we can't wait for North Korea*". The profits of her Lager Beer during the World Cup went to human rights organisations. Brewdog shows that you can challenge social norms with the power of your brand, and thus celebrate the fight against injustice statement after statement.

ROTTERDAM ZOO | VEGA CROQUETTE INCOGNITO

How can we make a statement with behavioural design?

For three years, anyone who ordered a croquette sandwich at the Rotterdam zoo Blijdorp was served a vegetarian and later even a vegan version. Apart from the brief green tick behind the word croquette, there was no explicit mention of it. According to the zoo, no visitor has ever noticed this. It's a well-known tactic in behavioural design: make the exception the default option. Rotterdam Zoo felt that a zoo was the right place to turn that logic around and celebrate the three-year social experiment as a media stunt. In time, all snacks in Blijdorp will become plant-based.

TUVALU | THE FIRST-EVER DIGITAL STATE

How do we bring risks in the future to the present to create urgency?

The independent island nation of Tuvalu in the Pacific Ocean is probably one of the most vulnerable nation-states that could be swallowed up by rising sea levels in the coming decades. To gain attention on the world stage, the nefarious plan was hatched to create a first digital state with the people of Tuvalu. Villages, houses, the whole cultural lore, myths, legends, scientific research into the unique fauna, flora and even the entire government administration would move to the metaverse. The plan was first proposed at COP27, where it was seen as a shock and disruptive precedent. After all, international law states that physical territory is a prerequisite for having a nation-state. Immediately, emergency funds were put on the agenda and digital Tuvalu was recognised by nine other countries to remain a functional state digitally.

'We need to practice
society's implicit richness on a daily basis.
Only then does it become generous
to us and beauty becomes something
you can find everywhere.'

———

HISTORIAN JACOB VOORTHUIS

ENERGY: THE HACKATHON AS A CELEBRATION OF SYSTEM CHANGE

*How moments of passionate pragmatism
can lead to system breakthroughs.*

A BREATHTAKING SUNRISE

We can agree that many developments with regard to the climate are far too slow. But if there's one trend that's consistently underestimated year after year, it's the rapid rise of solar energy. The IPCC's (United Nations Inter-governmental Panel on Climate Change) most optimistic scenario in 2014 assumed that solar power would cost about $885 per kilowatt by 2050, and that milestone was already reached in 2020. The dizzying power of innovation, coupled with Theodore Wright's law of 1936 (with every cumulative doubling of the number of units produced, the cost continues to fall steadily) continues to push solar energy forward in all graphs. From the IPCC to financial data analyst Bloomberg and the International Energy Agency, year after year they lag behind the exponential curve in their estimates. One wonders when or how the limit to growth will be reached. Maybe resource scarcity will put a stop to the party? In the production of solar energy, the availability of polysilicon has been a decisive factor in global production capacity. Thanks to the current catch-up in China, it is expected that the 1,100 gigawatts of installed capacity that will be operational worldwide in 2024 will become no less than 1,900 gigawatts by 2025. China will soon produce enough polysilicon to double its entire global production capacity in one year. Will there still be room for European players? Of course, all these solar cells have to be given a place and an application, which requires a lot of (highly and practically) trained personnel. In addition, there are all kinds of niches in the market with lucrative opportunities such as the production of lightweight, circular solar panels (Solarge from the Dutch municipality of Weert), flexible photovoltaic films (EnFoil from Hasselt in Belgium) or solar cells from perovskite (a completely different crystal than polysilicon) that can be printed on all possible surfaces such as window frames and roof windows of cars (Oxford Photovoltaics from the UK)

A nuclear reactor is a project,
a solar panel is a product.

Contrary to the prevailing green ideology, I was always in favour of nuclear energy. Belgium wants to build small nuclear reactors by 2040. The scenario of SMRs (small modular reactors) is promising, but in the energy sector itself you hear the question of whether this new generation of nuclear energy can still catch up with the solstice. According to the National Solar Trend Report 2024 (Dutch New Energy Research), solar energy is already two to three times cheaper than nuclear energy. And that's not even taking into account the uncertain supply lines of uranium from Russia, Kazakhstan, Niger, etc. Solar energy continues to climb the learning and innovation curve at a brisk pace uphill, while the price continues to thunder downhill. A nuclear reactor takes a long time to build, is a complex and expensive project. A solar panel is now a mass product, modular, and can even be found as a DIY kit at Ikea.

According to Dutch knowledge institutions such as TNO (Applied Scientific Research) and NPE (National Energy System Plan), the Netherlands is expected to produce 500 terawatt hours of renewable electricity by 2050 according to their current scenario exercises. That's 300 more than it will need with current growth projections. Despite this surplus, nuclear energy is often considered an important element in the energy mix within two decades to compensate for so-called *Dunkelflaute* (a combination of the German words 'Dunkelheit', which means darkness, and 'Flaute', which stands for little wind). But according to research by the Dutch operator of the high-voltage grid TenneT, it seems more and more likely that Dunkelflaute periods are getting shorter and shorter, and can also be compensated for with hydrogen and battery storage in the long term.

THE RELATIONSHIP BETWEEN PEOPLE AND ENERGY

Whatever the energy mix of tomorrow, we cannot reduce today's debate to an ideological debate about nuclear versus solar power. Nor can the energy transition be reduced to the switch from fossil energy to renewable. Yes, we need to move from heavy, expensive, flammable molecules to light, cheap, smart and obedient electrons. We agree on that. And if we look back in energy history, efficiency has always been better than waste, technology has always won out over raw materials, and economics has always won over ideology. The question is: how are we going to (re)distribute energy this time, with current technology? And how do we, as human beings, want to relate to energy?

- Will energy remain a kind of commodity in an economy with a price per kilowatt hour that is formed internationally and where investors continue to profit from price fluctuations?
- Or will energy become a system of networks in networks with free traffic – similar to the internet – where supply and demand are balanced as locally as possible and where every consumer can also be a producer?

A world where access to clean and affordable energy is a fundamental right is the goal to which impact entrepreneur Arash Aazami dedicates his entire passion, body and life. The creativity of two hundred interconnected professionals in hooded sweaters and laptops turns out to be greater than the imagination of people in suits and ties in meeting rooms. That is why he prefers to organise an annual energy hackathon where the energy transition is approached as a social system task.

Because you can't solve today's challenges with current logic, ideas and institutions, you need an informal, unorthodox, but professional setting where enlightened thinkers, creative souls, technical brains and ambitious dreamers find each other and design a new system like crusaders.

BUILDING BLOCKS OF A SUCCESSFUL HACKATHON

Arash's energy hackathons are always a feast of innovation with a few fixed ingredients:

1 **Pressure**
   An important ingredient is time pressure. A hackathon lasts a total of 48 hours and that ensures the accumulation of focus. All redundancy disappears and participants limit themselves to the essentials. That's why people often give their best creative performance when they don't have enough time for it.
2 **Carefully curated teams**
   A hackathon is preceded by an intensive process in which teams are put together and the major system challenges in the energy sector are discussed.

3 Meet-ups
This preliminary phase consists of a series of meet-ups. Digital
and physical meetings where urgency, challenges and process
are discussed.

4 System challenges
The so-called challenges are central to the hackathon. These are
always systemic challenges such as "how do we create a system where
more money is earned thanks to less energy" or "how do we integrate
car sharing to support energy sharing at district level?".

5 Challenge owners
The hackathon is made possible thanks to energy companies, grid operators, governments and knowledge institutions. It is important that
these '*regime players*' are also involved in the hackathon in terms of
content and operation, do not put the brakes on, but rather acknowledge the need for energy transition and help make it possible.

6 Jedis
Because the energy transition affects all sections of society, knowledge and inspiration from all kinds of disciplines is needed: urban planning, behavioural psychology, ecology, geology, physics, legislation,
etc. That's exactly why there are Jedi during hackathons: people who
have specific knowledge and experience to feed participating teams
with deeper system insights.

7 Design principles
Accessible to everyone, locally balancing, distributed system, spatially
integrated, ... At the heart of the hackathon is a set of design principles to ensure that teams come up with a rich variety of solutions,
but that fit into the purpose and spirit of the hackathon.

8 Unique location
The Transform Hackathon of 2022 took place in Fort Voordorp
in Utrecht, the Synergy Hackathon took place in the Green
Village at TU Delft, a place where energy technology is being
experimented with.

9 Follow-up process
The last hour of the hackathon is actually a new beginning. It is crucial
that the ideas find their way to maturity as soon as possible through
an impact booster trajectory or a series of safaris where participants
venture into streets and neighbourhoods in search of opportunities to
test their new ideas.

What if energy were as natural and freely accessible as the internet? To test the concept of an internet-of-energy against reality, Arash and his start-up Unify Energy are working with a Dutch telecom company and the residents of De Kleine Burg, a small residential area with *tiny houses* in Rotterdam. eleven small houses with big ideals … That is the ideal context to turn into an energy island. Here, research is being conducted into a whole new market model for energy: one in which all actors are rewarded for balance. In De Kleine Burg there are a total of 60 solar panels and there is a communal container of batteries, inverters and an electric car that can charge and discharge energy. If the telecom company uses its internet-of-things capabilities by having all these devices talk to each other and share energy, that energy demand no longer has to run past the meter, and you help grid operators relieve the energy network. In this way, you effectively create an anti-energy company: you decimate energy demand in the market, reduce the difference between supply and demand and reward balance at the neighbourhood level. What Arash wants to demonstrate with De Kleine Brug is that you can affordably meet up to 80% of the energy demand yourself thanks to local connection. In doing so, he implements European directives from the bottom up that focus on 'collective self-consumption': energy independence thanks to connection.

PASSIONATE PRAGMATISM

During a meeting at the Eye Film Museum in Amsterdam, I was very impressed by the Dutch systemic therapist Steven Pont. During a full-length performance, he managed to entertain the audience with just one Power-Point slide at the ready. In unashamed Windows 95 style, he showed that in every organisation there is a "formal, rational upper current" with all kinds of things that are conceived in a meeting room: the mission, the vision, the values of the company, the KPIs, the annual planning, etc. but also the job descriptions, corporate brochures, the annual financial report and the sustainability report. In that formal upstream, that organisation usually looks immaculate and fantastic. He points out that the real strength of an organisation lies in its "emotional, informal and undefined undercurrent": What are the stories and sentiment at the coffee machine? What do people get out of bed for? Can people express the best of themselves? Or have they long since decided not to show their talent anymore? The real system is ingrained in the organsational culture and will only flourish if it has a beckoning perspective and is willing to provide space for the talent that is there. There is a lot of drive, vision and passion in the energy sector. But enlightened minds often feel lonely there. The organisations they work for have been self-sustaining for too long. But in the meantime, more and more people are wondering why there is an energy supplier between their refrigerator and solar panel. A hackathon is an informal setting and context where talent with new ideas can find each other and passionate pragmatism is given free rein. The result is not only the new system solutions, but also the fluid network that manages to find each other permanently across the borders of companies and sectors after they have experienced an unforgettable creative trip together.

'You never change things by fighting
against the existing reality.
To change something,
build a new model
that makes the existing model obsolete.'

RICHARD BUCKMINSTER FULLER,
ARCHITECT, AUTHOR, INVENTOR AND PHILOSOPHER

NINE IMPRESSIVE EXAMPLES OF FRONTRUNNERS IN THE ENERGY TRANSITION

SOLARVILLE | MAKING THE MICROGRID CHILDISHLY ACCESSIBLE

How do we make our provo type as accessible as a toy?

Worldwide, 770 million people live without electricity. To achieve universal access by 2030, 100 million people need to be connected each year. But reaching these homes with cumbersome, outdated, and centralised energy networks is slow, expensive, and logistically difficult in many countries. Moreover, these systems are usually still entangled in fossil logic. Space 10, Ikea's former innovation hub, therefore came up with Solarville: a miniature wooden village on a scale of 1:50 that looks like a box of blocks and represents a smart energy network at district level. Here, people produce energy together, and share it automatically. The model intentionally makes the complex system childishly accessible: you can observe a fully functional network of blockchain-traded energy and interact with a lamp as an artificial sun to understand its effects on the network in real time.

SCHOONSCHIP | FLOATING OFF-THE-GRID LIVING

What if a citizens' collective manages to escape real estate logic?

Schoonschip, which claims to be the most sustainable floating district in Europe, started with one woman's desire to live. She wanted to *live comfortably off-the-grid* in a full-fledged home on the water. Soon, other citizens joined in. And so, in a short period of time, a group of like-minded Dutch people became the client for something that had never happened before. Today, about fifty different houses float on individual pontoons in the Johan van Hasselt Canal in Amsterdam-Noord. The houses each have a different designer, but all consist of circular materials with a material passport. All roofs carry a total of five hundred solar panels and the district has its own *smart grid* to exchange energy. Heat and electricity are mutually billed with their own cryp-tocurrency, the Joulliette. The local residents have their own fleet of shared cars and work in floating greenhouses to grow their own vegetables.

NOVAR | SOLAR PARKING SPACES AND PHOTOVOLTAIC COW PASTURES

How can we shift competition for open space to collaboration?

It is better to produce energy as close as possible to where it is needed. This prevents further congestion on the already overloaded energy network, es-pecially now that we are pumping more renewable energy into the grid every year and using more electric cars. The Dutch company Novar offers a smart business model and a spatially intelligent approach by providing parking spaces with a solar roof. Solar roofs provide shade and shelter from the rain to parking lots, while energy is generated from the sun, right where cars are charged. For the Lowlands music festival, Novar built the largest solar carport in the world with no less than 90,000 panels. France passed a law at the end of 2022 that requires solar panels above above-ground parking lots in eighty or more parking spaces. The Netherlands has included this obligation in its 2023 Environment and Planning Act.

ECODORP BOEKEL | IN-VIVO RESEARCH FOR ECOLOGICAL DISTRICTS

What if the new neighbourhood in your municipality becomes a living lab?

Walls of lime and hemp, cementless concrete, wastewater purified in reeds... Ecovillage Boekel is one big in-vivo experiment of ecological innovation for housing. Residents sign a contract that they agree to act as guinea pigs. A special example of innovation is the basalt battery of the 75-year-old inventor Cees van Nimwegen, which stores energy in a battery of metal, rock wool and basalt stone and thus provides heat and hot water to 36 homes. Insurers involved, such as Achmea and Interpolis, are also experimenting with it. Insurance and lending for innovations are difficult because the risks are unprecedented. Interpolis sees its green roofs as a prevention solution that reduces water damage, is good for biodiversity and roofs that last longer.

Boekel is a place where they also innovate and can claim a leading position by experimenting.

ZERO BILLS HOMES |
GUARANTEE OF ZERO ENERGY COSTS

What if energy companies and project developers build a neighbourhood together?

Energy company Octopus Energy and Bellway, one of the UK's largest house builders, are teaming up to build homes with a zero energy cost guarantee. Residents can easily save £1,800 a year as a family. Family homes will be equipped with heat pumps, solar panels and home batteries and will be scaled on the Octopus Kraken Platform, an intelligent energy network. A first pilot with 250 houses in the town of Bedfordshire should show the world that it can be done. After that, the coalition wants to build 50,000 Zero Bills homes by 2025.

QIRION | ENERGY ISLANDS
WITH SEAWATER BATTERIES

What if old energy infrastructure becomes the basis for the new one?

The Netherlands is expected to benefit from 11.5 gigawatts of offshore wind energy by 2030 … But for wind-quiet days, a surprising plan awaits in the Dutch province of Zeeland. Atolls are ring-shaped energy islands where nature is combined with coastal protection, food production, floating solar panels and energy storage in thousands of saltwater batteries below the water level. A seawater battery is a large bag of water with three separate compartments. Membranes ensure that salt water is split into acidic and alkaline water. When offshore wind farms do not yield anything, the water is mixed back in and energy is released. In this way, the artificial inland seas of the atolls become the rechargeable batteries of the Netherlands. To show how it works, Qirion has already built one such island in the estuary of the Western Scheldt. After comparative research, the University of Twente came to the conclusion that saltwater storage requires up to twice as much space, energy and materials as a comparable island with hydrogen storage. That is why saltwater batteries are receiving more and more attention today to be used as home batteries.

CEMVITA | ORGANIC HYDROGEN FARMS IN ABANDONED OIL FIELDS

What if we learn to see a spectrum of opportunities between grey and green?

In the world of hydrogen, there are different colours: green hydrogen from solar and wind energy, blue from natural gas, and grey from other fossil fuels. After experiments in the lab, as well as experiments in an empty oil well in West Texas, they are making a case for producing hydrogen at a fraction of the price, possibly as little as $1 per kilogram. This is done by injecting hungry bacteria into abandoned oil fields, where they eat the remaining hydrocarbons and excrete hydrogen and CO_2. Despite its enormous potential with the world's many abandoned oil fields, it also raises questions about its ecological impact and alleged CO_2 storage.

POWERNESTS | HYBRID ROOFTOP INSTALLATIONS OF WIND AND SOLAR ENERGY

What if the roofs of office buildings become the new energy fields?

More and more people are seeking refuge in the city, society is moving away from fossil fuels, mobility is electrifying and buildings are becoming taller. As a result, solar panels on the roof are less and less sufficient to provide all residents of a building with the necessary power. At the same time, regulations in Europe are pushing new construction more and more towards energy neutrality. To cope with this field of tension, Eindhoven-based Ibis Power developed a roof window, or *'power nest'* consisting of a combination of wind turbines and solar panels to provide high-rise buildings with up to ten times more self-produced electricity. The first powernest demos can be seen on the roof of the Zadkin college in Rotterdam, Valkenburg airport in Katwijk aan Zee and on the residential complex Eden district in Rotterdam and Haasje Over in Eindhoven.

MAANA ELECTRIC | AUTONOMOUS AND IN-SITU PRODUCTION OF ENERGY CAPACITY

What if we have to produce energy,
only with what is abundantly available locally?

How can we provide humans with energy wherever they go in our solar system? With its Terrabox and Lunabox, Luxembourg-based Maana Electric is developing microfactories that allow you to produce ISRU solar panels fully automatically wherever you can find sand. ISRU stands for 'In-Situ Resource Utilisation'. Maana Electric is, to my knowledge, the only organisation that offers a solid answer to the question: how are we going to power extraterrestrial colonies? One such Lunabox can produce as much as 1 megawatt of solar capacity per year from regolith (the loose, dusty sand on celestial bodies such as Mars or the moon). A machine that eats sand and defecates solar panels... It goes without saying that these microfactories on earth can also do meaningful work. Much of what we need to live on Mars can be put to good use to ensure the continuity of life on Earth.

EPILOGUE AND ACKNOWL- EDGEMENTS

Writing a book is always a bit provotyping for me. It starts with an urge that manifests itself in collecting mania and stacking zeal. The many perspectives of sky-stormers, cross-thinkers, enterprising crusaders, troublemakers and geniuses lead to a multifaceted and kaleidoscopic picture of the future full of abrasive contradictions, but also special encounters and new bonds that deserve to be celebrated. It is thanks to Marije Roefs, Sabrine den Os, Niels Janssens, Cami Vanstapel and Klaartje Ballon at LannooCampus that this writing has been a streamlined process and four months of listening, puzzling, drawing and writing has taken the form of a book. Thanks also to Mieke Geenen, with whom we *came up with the captivating illustrations in this book in real We, Myself & A.I. mode, and also a deep bow to my best friend Olaf Meuleman who, as a celebrated creative director, also took the time to oversee the creative expressions in this book.*

And then, of course, the many heroes and heroines whose stories are often enacted in this book after a cup of coffee or a meeting in the field: Ap Verheggen with his SunGlacier, Janine Geijsen from Spacebuzz, Raffael-Leonardo Broy from Coral Cousins and Komang Karya, the guardians of the coral reef on the coast of Nusa Penida, Jessica den Outer for your unique fight for rights for nature. Michael Humblet, Feline Godon, Jan Leyssens and Stéphane Vanden Broeck for the generosity with which you share your boundless knowledge and experience. Milan Meyberg, to show how we can use AI to teach society to talk to nature, Arash Aazami, to give us a feast of passionate pragmatism and to bring the internet-of-energy ever closer. Koert Van Mensvoort and Nina Monfils of Next Nature for your inspiration on future exploration and inspiring lines of thought on the future of technology and nature, Thomas D'hooge, for your fight for future literacy, Herman Konings, to welcome me to your Theatre of Tales for that extra shot of trends and inspiration. Jaap Seil, Ioana Dobrescu and Jacob Bossaer for your commitment to the absolute life support system of the planet: water. Jaap Korteweg of Those Vegan Cowboys and Lucas De Man of Stichting Nieuwe Helden for your mastery of storytelling. Siviglia Berto, Ellen Van Den Brande, Rik Menten, Louis De Jaegher, Elena Doms, Frederik Verstraete and Piet Opstaele for your courage, drive, leadership and entrepreneurial strength. Nadina Galle, Cécil Konijnendijk, Koos Biesmeijer, Joost Verhaegen 'alias De Boominee' and Linda Kessler to take the debate on green infrastructure to a higher level. Michel Scholte, Tom De Bruyne, Rutger Bregman, to be a permanent inspiration with your podcasts, columns, lectures, books and media interventions. Not only in terms of content, but also the courage and flair with which you propagate your field and struggles give so much energy and ideas. A very special mention is also in order for Astrid Leyssens and the entire crew of 'We Are Impact Collective', a family in the making without borders. And let's not forget the colleagues at Love Tomorrow: Joris Beckers, Jonas Steyaert, Mats Raes, Nina de Man, Juliette Broucke, Jeroen Franssen and Jan Van den Broeck, another family thanks to whom I have an extra window open on the world.

But what would I be without my daughter Juliette, my – now – wife Judith Clijsters and my son Casper, who was born right in the middle of this writing process. All love for you, thank you for the space I get to write books and all my other whims.

And you, dear reader. I hope that you will use this book as a kind of tool until it is worn to the seam. I hope that you will join me in defying natural laws and assumptions as you do with new ideas: the more we share them, the more they multiply.

Only by absorbing apparent contradictions with creativity can we travel the road from the old normal to the new sublime!

With deep bow,

Stefaan

THE BEAUTY IS HIDDEN
IN THE INTENTION

It is Wednesday, January 19, 1983. The then BRT (Belgian Radio and Television) brought about a true television revolution in the then, grey, Flemish television landscape. The programme *IJsbreker* (*Icebreaker*) of the Department of Art Affairs offered a surprising look at television that can best be described as a live video installation. So on TV ... In many living rooms still in black and white.

Like a Teams meeting *avant la lettre*, three locations in Flanders are connected to each other via a radio link. In the living room of journalist and poet Georges Adé in Mechelen, Professor of Philosophy of Science Herman Roelants joins the camera. In an editing room at the BRT, the director and the Brussels professor of Mechanics Charles Hirsch take a seat, while artist Panamarenko is accompanied by his elderly mother in his living room-studio at Biekorfstraat 2 in the Seefhoek, a working-class district of Antwerp.

The aim of the broadcast: to subject Panamarenko's work to a scientific review. People ask questions that must have made the '*Leonardo Da Vinci of the City*' tire all his life: Does this really work? And can this really fly?

Panamarenko holds his own during the critical interrogation of the academics. The poet and philosopher of the company are equally enchanted by Panamareko's magical exposition on the anatomy of hymenopteran insects. The rig demonstrated by Panamarenko was visibly inspired by insects. When the philosopher politely asks if the device is actually capable of making an insect flight, the artist gives an answer that the company doesn't know what to do with: "Oooh but I don't know... Because you have to have a very, very long time for that. Insects have taken millions of years to do this. I don't have that much time. For me, it is enough if I have found an insight about it thanks to my work. If we can learn something from them."

A palpable shake-up of the spirit occurs in the studio. Afterwards, the professor of Mechanics shares his aha moment with television-watching Flanders: "For the artist, it is sufficient to dig up an insight and reveal it to an audience. It is only in the next step that engineers, money and time are brought in. That's when we step out of the art world and into the field of science and technology."

The balance is restored in the broadcast. Because there had just been a film fragment in which Panamarenko makes an unsuccessful attempt to air christen his *airomodeller* (a kind of zepellin) on a meadow to fly it from the Flemish Kempen to The Hague. We heard the reporter's scornful comment about eighty thousand Belgian francs of public money going up in the air. But after the broadcast, Panamarenko no longer seems like a bubble blower, a pipe dreamer, a weirdo or a charlatan.

Although what he does most closely resembles *play*: the beauty lies hidden in the intention, not in the result. Thanks to that beauty, all his creations, attempts or alleged failures have the power to sustain imagination and progress.

'The meaning of existence
is the accumulation
of poetic moments.'

———

THE THREEFOLD WISDOM
OF THE TREE

See the Leaves
The wisdom of change
Letting go again and again

See the branches
The wisdom of growth
Longing again and again

See the roots
The wisdom of volmulation
Again and again deepening

CELTIC TRIAD FROM AROUND 1100

SOURCE LIST

https://stefaanvandist.eu/provotyping-
research-and-resources-for-the-book/

ILLUSTRATIONS AND PHOTOS

With a few exceptions, all illustrations in this book are the result of an intriguing collaboration with Mieke Geenen. Here, I give her the floor to talk about the creative process she calls AI-whispering.

AI-WHISPERING

Since I began working as a freelance photoshopper around 2002, the world of image manipulation has rapidly transformed. The practical implications for my work are significant. Apps are updated because there's a new, faster solution for something, I follow geeks on social media, and I watch YouTube videos about the latest tools.

While the debate continues about the value of the human hand, the charm of imperfection, the pace of a creative process, ethical questions, and so on, I explore generative art. Every time someone passionately defends the craft of drawing against the machine, I understand very well what they mean, as a former student of painting and analog photography. There is an irreplaceable interweaving with time and reality. The experience of making can be somewhat recalled by the viewer; you can almost hear the scratching of the pencil on an unfinished work.

It's unlikely that, when viewing an AI-generated piece, you'll ponder the sound of a prompt being typed. Generative AI images simply appear soundlessly from one second to the next. I'm not going to call it a renaissance; I'm mostly very curious about other and new ways to create an image. When Stefaan asked if I could create AI illustrations for his book, I immediately said yes. What he writes about is also situated somewhere in a chaotic trajectory without a perfect endpoint, in a human evolution that happens entirely in interaction with technology, in new possible permutations.

Stefaan describes the idea. I engage in AI-whispering and formulate as best as possible what the result should be: colors, perspective, style... until something comes out of the machine that I can use as a starting image. Often, I watch the developing image with fascination, especially when I input a spectacular prompt like a coral city, a Panamarenko spacecraft, or futuristic-vintage recyclable plastic. No matter how wondrous the images are, they are never quite as you had envisioned them in your imagination. That's why I combine images in Photoshop, finishing them further. In the end, I remove the AI glitches and adjust the colors. It is a unique and enjoyable process; I am very grateful to Stefaan for trusting the outcome of my interaction with this emerging technology

OPENING
- FUTURE TOWER, Cover image Mieke Geenen for Provotyping
- TOUCH, own work by Mieke Geenen
- Public Speaking 2022-2024, Stefaan Vandist
- BIAS, Mieke Geenen for Provotyping

7 REASONS WHY SUSTAINABILITY DOESN'T WORK
- AVALANCHE, own work by Mieke Geenen
- CHARCOAL, Mieke Geenen for Provotyping
- BOARDING, Mieke Geenen for Provotyping

7+1 SUPERPOWERS
- TOTEM BUNNIES, own work by Mieke Geenen
- BRAIN SCAN, Mieke Geenen for Provotyping
- GATHERING, Mieke Geenen for Provotyping
- IMMUNE, Mieke Geenen for BioOrg

- ICE CASTLE, own work by Mieke Geenen
- SUNGLACIER DUBAI, supplied by Ap Verheggen
- OVERVIEW EFFECT, Mieke Geenen for Provotyping
- CORAL METROPOLIS, Mieke Geenen for Provotyping
- Coral Classes, Nuansa Pulau Nusa Penida 2023, Stefaan Vandist
- PLASTIC PACKAGING, Mieke Geenen for Provotyping
- ONIONS, Mieke Geenen for Provotyping
- EMISSARY OF GAIA, Milan Meyberg
- Workshops 2022-2024, Stefaan Vandist & Jan Leyssens
- Baloise Learning Experience 2022-2023, B-Tonic
- HAPPY COIN, Mieke Geenen for Provotyping

WHAT IF
- ATOMIC ENERGY LAB, Mieke Geenen for Provotyping
- MOTHER EARTH, Mieke Geenen for Provotyping
- DROPSTORE, Mieke Geenen for Provotyping
- SUSHI CUBES, Mieke Geenen for Provotyping
- FOREST PLATE, Mieke Geenen for Provotyping
- ROBOT BURGER, Mieke Geenen for Provotyping

COALITION OF THE WILLING
- HEMP FIELD, Mieke Geenen for Provotyping
- SUPERHEROES, Mieke Geenen for Provotyping
- DIATOMS, own work by Mieke Geenen
- TJOKVOL, supplied by New Horizon
- AQUA FARMING, Mieke Geenen for Provotyping
- Workshop Steerer 2023, Stefaan Vandist & Jan Leyssens
- Oceanix, supplied by Bjarke ingels Group

PROVOTYPING
- MICROBIAL VENDING, Mieke Geenen for Provotyping
- MYCOSHOE, Mieke Geenen for Provotyping
- BIODIGITAL TREE, Mieke Geenen for Provotyping
- TREES ON WHEELS, Mieke Geenen for Provotyping
- GREEN LIGHT DISTRICT, Mieke Geenen for Provotyping
- BRIXTON VILLAGE, Wouter Van Vaerenbergh for We, Myself & A.I.
- SMART STREET, Wouter Van Vaerenbergh for We, Myself & A.I.
- MODULAR MAILBOX, Mieke Geenen for Provotyping

CELEBRATION
- SOLARPUNK FESTIVAL, Mieke Geenen for Provotyping
- SUPERKILEN PARK, supplied by Bjarke ingels Group
- MYSTIC FOREST, Mieke Geenen for Provotyping
- SOLARVILLE, Mieke Geenen for Provotyping
- PANAMARENKO, Mieke Geenen for Provotyping
- MAGIC TREE, Mieke Geenen for Provotyping

END
- EARTH MASK, Mieke Geenen for Provotyping

STEP 2

AMMO CHAMBER
What are the key skills, resources, and strengths we need to realise our vision?

ALLIES
Who are the 'usual suspects', but especially the 'unusual suspects' for our alliance?

COALITION OF THE WILLING

To go to war, you need an army. With a 'coalition of the willing' you create your own power of change.

CASE BELLI
What are both the barriers and drivers of our potential allies to join?

THE STRONGHOLD
Which location would be the best strategic position for our 'coalition of the willing'?

OUR PIONEERING ALLIANCE
How would you name our 'coalition of the willing'?